Editorial Project Manager
Lorin E. Klistoff, M.A.

Editor in Chief
Ina Massler Levin, M.A.

Illustrator
Kelly McMahon

Cover Artist
Brenda DiAntonis

Creative Director
Karen J. Goldfluss, M.S. Ed.

Art Production Manager
Kevin Barnes

Art Coordinator
Renée Christine Yates

Imaging
James Edward Grace
Craig Gunnell

Publisher

Mary D. Smith, M.S. Ed.

Authors

Franka Chavez-Rodriguez,

Mayra Saenz-Ulloa, M.A.,

and Sabrina Mastromarco-Diaz

Teacher Created Resources, Inc.
6421 Industry Way
Westminster, CA 92683
www.teachercreated.com

ISBN: 978-1-4206-2077-1

© 2008 Teacher Created Resources, Inc.

Made in U.S.A.

Table of Contents

 # Table of Contents *(cont.)*

Introduction

Reading is essentially the fundamental tool to all academic success. *Word Family Activities: Long Vowels* addresses the standards for reading skills, while assisting test preparation in enriching and creative ways. In recent years, there has been an increasingly strong emphasis on teaching word families in the primary curriculum in order to meet the demands of developing fluent readers. This book addresses the K–1 grade level, and the activities are extremely teacher/student friendly. It is designed with large print for young learners, along with simple identifiable pictures to help assist English language learners. The activities in part 1 are designed to build student success in word family knowledge using a very basic understanding. This allows proper scaffolding to take place during a teacher's instruction. Part 2 activities lead into challenging the learner's knowledge during student independent work time. This section allows the learner to manipulate the sounds in each of the word families. Part 3 ensures that students are able to read, write, and identify word families. Additional resources are also included to further assist instruction.

Standards

Word Family Activities: Long Vowels meets the following language arts standard and benchmarks for the K–1 grades classroom. (Used with permission from McREL. Copyright 2004 McREL. Mid-Continent Research for Educational and Learning. 2550 S. Parker Road, Suite 500, Aurora, CO 80014. Telephone: (303) 337-0990. Website: www.mcrel.org/standards-benchmarks.)

Standard 5: Uses the general skills and strategies of the reading process

- Uses basic elements of phonetic analysis (e.g., common letter/sound relationships, beginning and ending consonants, vowel sounds, blends, word patterns) to decode unknown words

- Uses basic elements of structural analysis (e.g., syllables, basic prefixes, suffixes, root words, compound words, spelling patterns, contractions) to decode unknown words

---

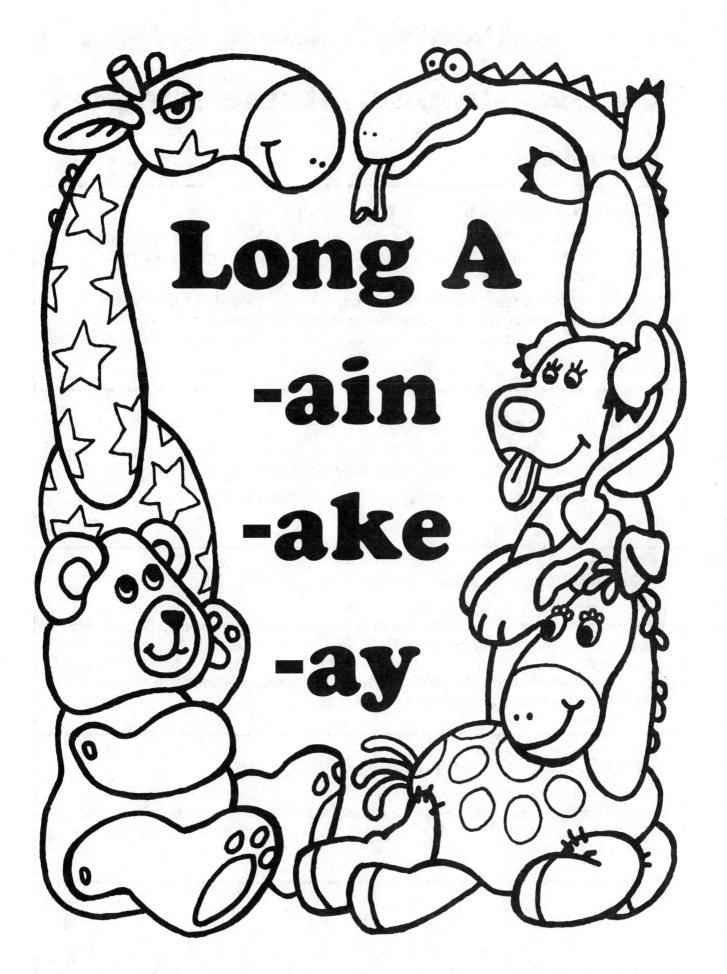

Long A
-ain
-ake
-ay

Part 1: Long A
Teacher Support/Home Support

Activity Directions

Flashcards (pages 7–8, pages 9–10, or pages 11–12)

Copy the set of flashcards that you want the students to learn back to back (pages 7 and 8, pages 9 and 10, or pages 11 and 12). Make sure the cards align properly when copying.

Have students trace and rewrite "long a" words on side A along with reading the words aloud. Side B will allow students to draw their own interpretations of the words. Students will then cut out the cards and place them on a ring for review or use them as a reference.

Letter Slide (page 13, 14, or 15)

Teacher precuts dashed lines inside the pictures. Students will cut the strips of letters. Students insert the letter strips to create and manipulate "long a" words.

(*Note:* Students can independently ask other classmates to read the words created with the letter slide.)

Blending Boxes (page 16, 17, or 18)

First, inform students that they will be building words by listening for beginning, middle, and ending sounds. Next, the teacher stretches out the words. Both student and teacher repeat the word slowly. Then, the teacher will ask questions to help guide the students to develop the sounds to write in the proper boxes. Lastly, students blend the sounds while connecting the dots to show directionality. Students read the words and practice writing them on the line.

Beginning Sound Substitution (page 19, 20, or 21)

Students cross out the beginning sound to create a new "long a" word. Use the pictures on the left as a guide. Have students read the words as they create them. Teacher must inform students that they are only substituting the beginning sound to create new words.

chain

pain

Spain

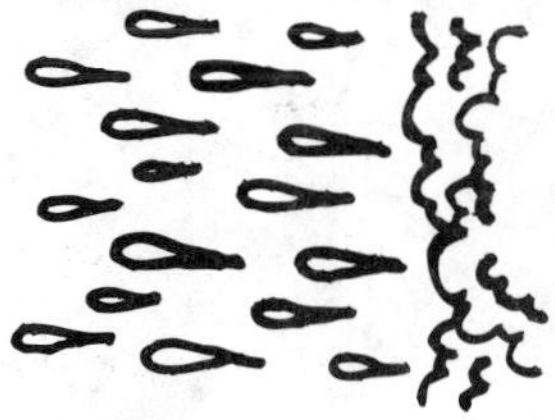

rain

train

brain

Side B

pain	chain
rain	Spain
brain	train

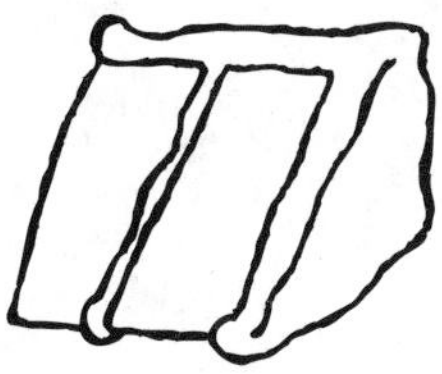

flake

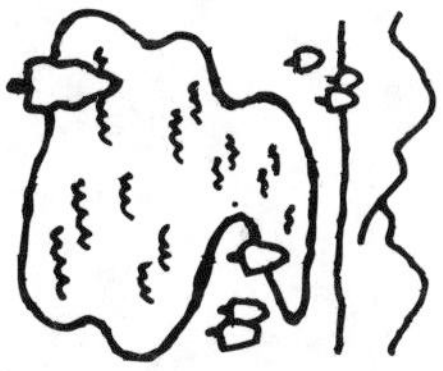

cake

shake

lake

snake

rake

Side B

cake

flake

lake

shake

rake

snake

gray

day

play

ray

spray

say

day

gray

ray

play

say

spray

12

Letter Slide

Cut the strip of letters. Cut the slits on the train. Insert the strip of letters to create and manipulate the **-ain** words.

| p | br | ch | Sp | tr | r |

_ _ _ _ ain

Letter Slide

Cut the strip of letters. Cut the slits on the cake. Insert the strip of letters to create and manipulate the **–ake** words.

c i r fl sh sn

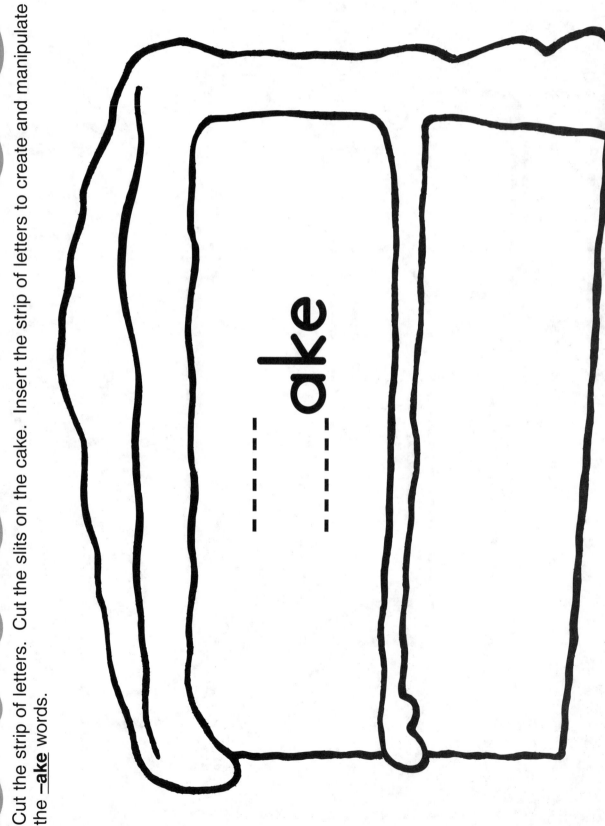

_ _ _ ake

Letter Slide

Cut the strip of letters. Cut the slits on the sun. Insert the strip of letters to create and manipulate the **–ay** words.

_ _ _ _ _ _ _
_ _ _ _ _ _ ay

d
r
s
gr
pl
spr

Blending Boxes

Blending Boxes

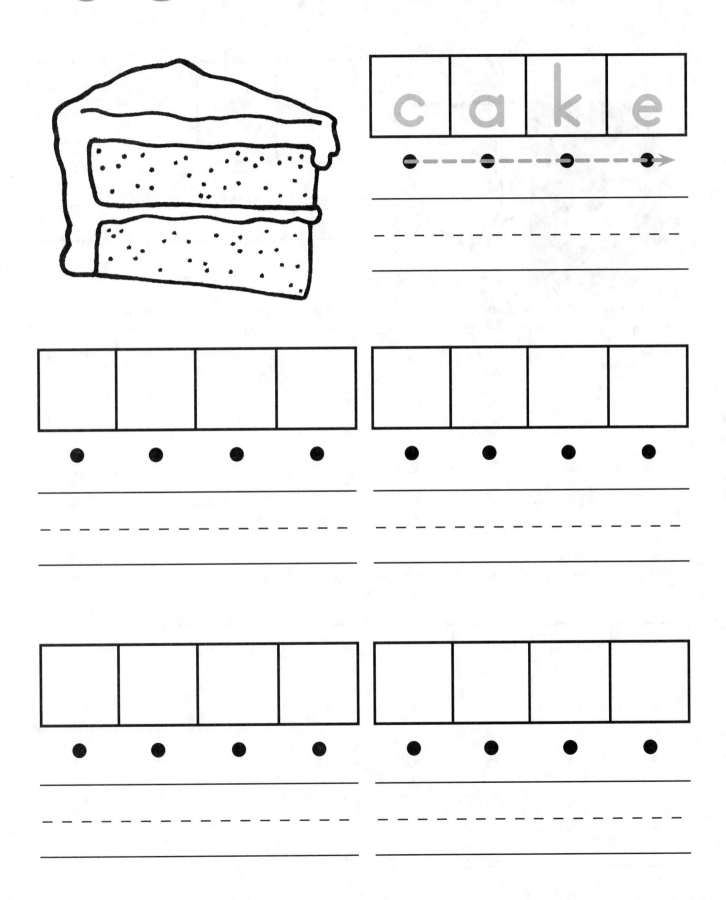

Blending Boxes

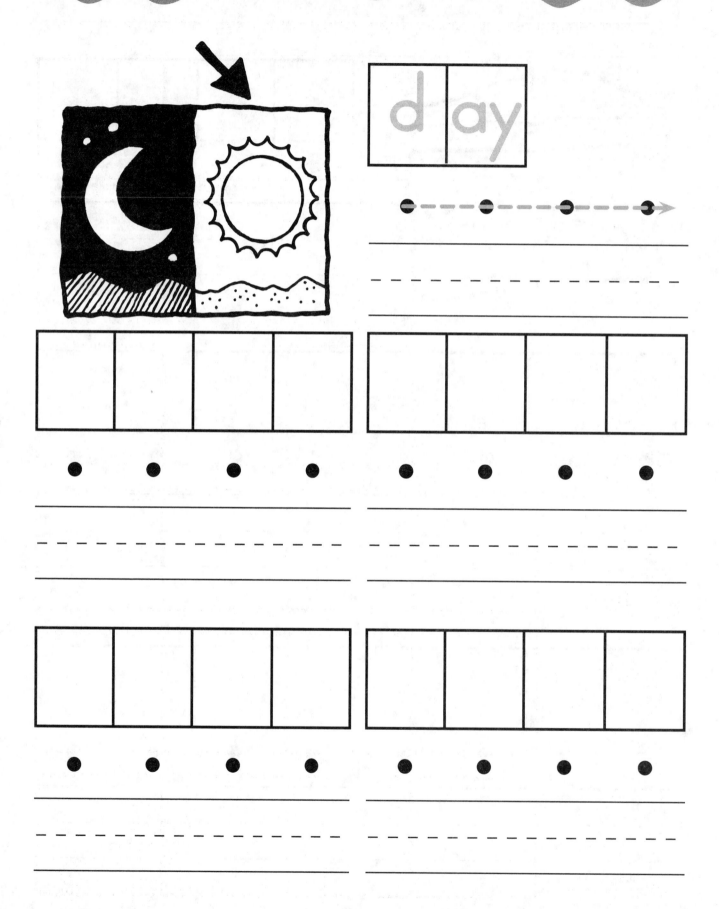

Beginning Sound Substitution

Cross out the beginning sound to create a new **–ain** word. Use the pictures on the left as a guide.

Beginning Sound Substitution

Cross out the beginning sound to create a new **–ake** word. Use the pictures on the left as a guide.

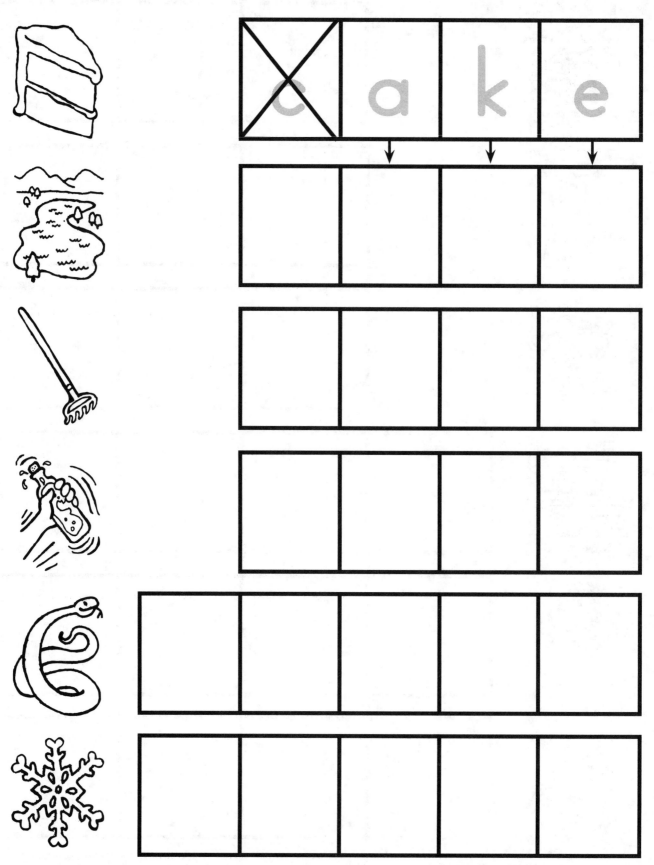

Beginning Sound Substitution

Cross out the beginning sound to create a new **–ay** word. Use the pictures on the left as a guide.

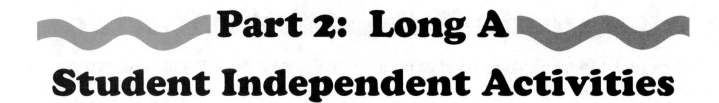

Part 2: Long A
Student Independent Activities

Activity Directions

Building Words (page 23, 24, or 25)

Cut out the letter boxes. Glue the letters in the correct boxes to create words that match the corresponding pictures.

Flip Book (pages 26–28 for *–ain*, pages 29–31 for *–ake*, or pages 32–34 for *–ay*)

Copy page 2 and the "My Picture" page back to back. Make sure the dashed lines are aligned. Then copy page 1.

First, fold page 2 along the solid line and only cut the dashed lines.

Second, cut and glue the pictures from page 1 onto the flip book (page 2).

Third, have students draw their own pictures where it says "My Picture" in the inside.

Fourth, cut out the letter boxes from page 1. Glue letters to the corresponding pictures to make the correct words.

Fifth, have students write the words two more times.

Mystery Picture (page 35, 36, or 37)

Find and color the "long a" words to discover the mystery picture. Once the mystery picture is discovered, students will then write the "long a" mystery word in the sentence below.

Word Search (page 38, 39, or 40)

Find and color the "long a" words. Have students write the "long a" words that are found in the word search in the empty spaces below.

Building Words

Cut out the letters below. Glue them in the correct boxes to create words that match the **–ain** pictures.

Building Words

Cut out the letters below. Glue them in the correct boxes to create words that match the **–ake** pictures.

Building Words

Cut out the letters below. Glue them in the correct boxes to create words that match the **–ay** pictures.

Flip Book (–ain)

Cut out the pictures and letters below.

Glue them on the flip book.

fold

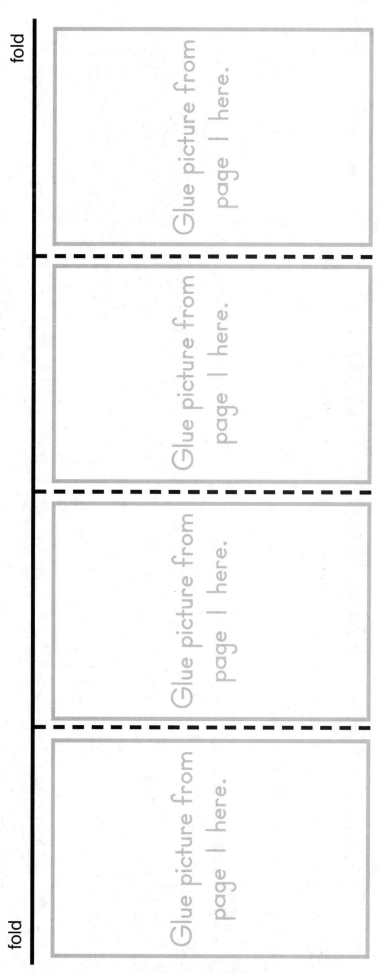

Glue picture from page 1 here.

Glue picture from page 1 here.

Glue picture from page 1 here.

Glue picture from page 1 here.

fold

My Picture

My Picture

My Picture

My Picture

ain

ain

ain

ain

Page 2

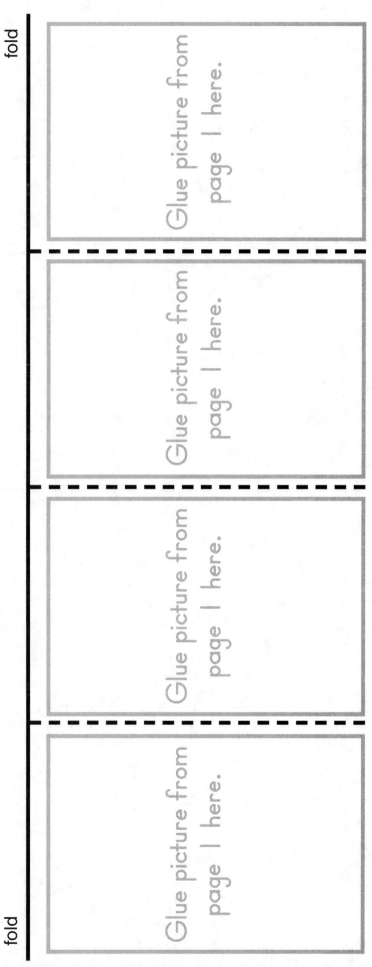

fold

Glue picture from
page 1 here.

Glue picture from
page 1 here.

Glue picture from
page 1 here.

Glue picture from
page 1 here.

fold

#2077 Word Family Activities: Long Vowels

My Picture	_ake
My Picture	_ake
My Picture	_ake
My Picture	_ake

Flip Book (–ake)

Cut out the pictures and letters below.

Glue them on the flip book.

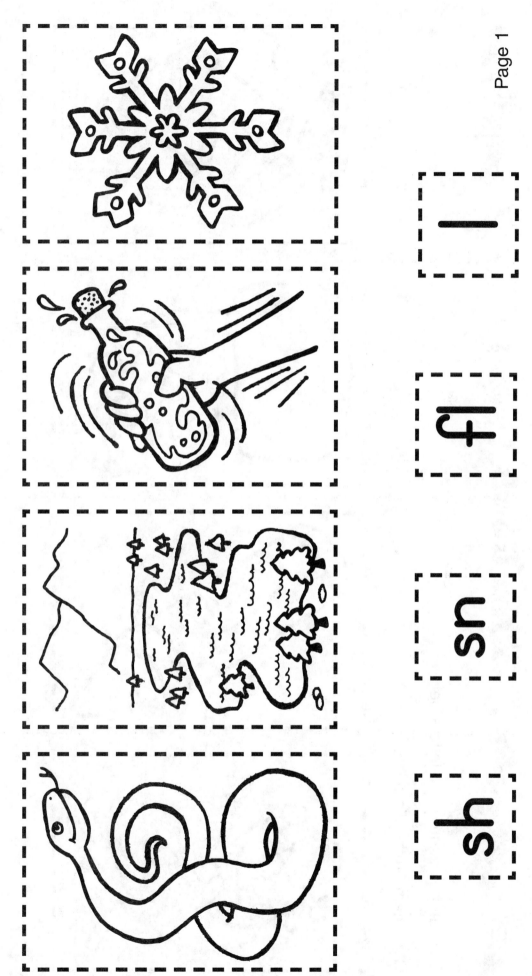

31   *#2077 Word Family Activities: Long Vowels*

Flip Book (−ay)

Cut out the pictures and letters below.

Glue them on the flip book.

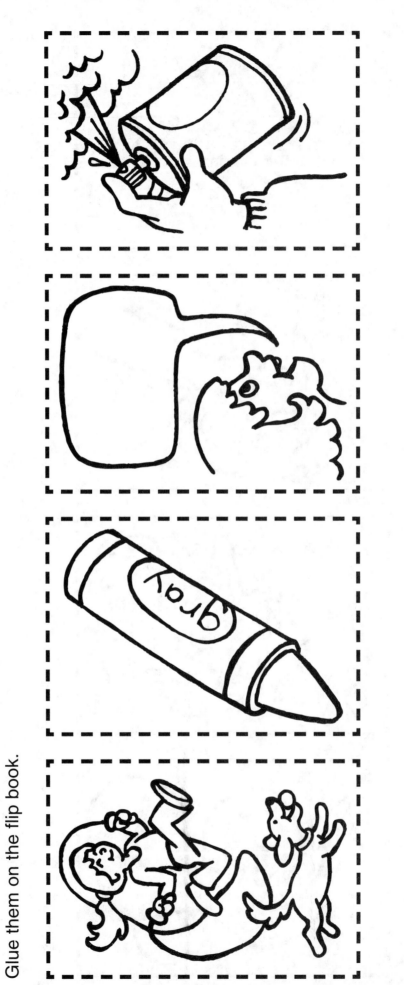

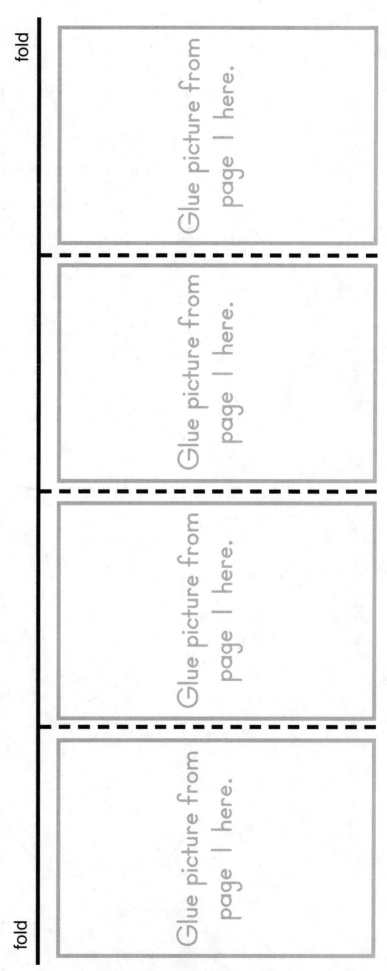

fold

Glue picture from page 1 here.

Glue picture from page 1 here.

Glue picture from page 1 here.

Glue picture from page 1 here.

fold

My Picture

My Picture

My Picture

My Picture

ay

ay

ay

ay

Mystery Picture

Color the spaces with the **–ain** pictures blue to discover the mystery picture.
Color the other spaces brown.

We enjoy the _____ !

 # Mystery Picture

Color the spaces with the **–ake** pictures pink to discover the mystery picture.
Color the other spaces yellow.

Where is my _____?

Color the spaces with the **–ay** pictures gray to discover the mystery picture. Color the other spaces green.

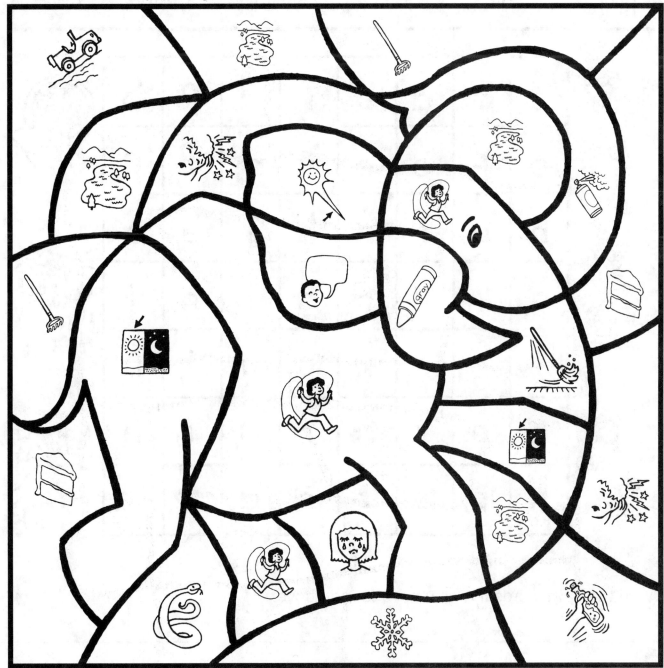

This animal is _____.

Word Search

Find and color the **–ain** words.

pain	rain	brain	chain	Spain	train

c	f	a	b	r	d	p	S
c	p	c	e	u	m	f	p
h	a	f	n	h	t	e	a
a	i	q	r	a	i	n	i
i	n	s	k	u	u	t	n
n	e	z	b	r	a	i	n
h	p	e	t	r	a	i	n

Write the **–ain** words that you have found above.

_____   _____   _____

_____   _____   _____

_____   _____   _____

_____   _____   _____

Word Search

Find and color the **–ake** words.

cake	lake	rake	flake	shake	snake

c	a	k	e	e	d	p	l
c	m	c	f	u	m	f	a
s	r	f	l	h	t	e	k
n	e	q	a	r	a	k	e
a	n	s	h	a	k	e	n
k	a	k	e	b	g	z	e
e	f	l	a	k	e	a	d

Write the **–ake** words that you have found above.

_____   _____   _____

_____   _____   _____

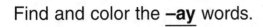

Word Search

Find and color the **–ay** words.

day	ray	say	gray	play	spray

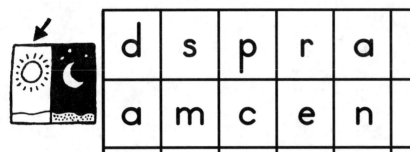

d	s	p	r	a	y	e	t
a	m	c	e	n	e	t	e
y	w	f	b	h	t	e	d
a	w	q	e	r	t	h	g
n	t	s	t	a	u	t	r
p	l	a	y	y	g	z	a
h	f	s	a	y	t	a	y

Write the **–ay** words that you have found in the word search.

_____   _____   _____

_____   _____   _____

_____   _____   _____

Part 3: Long A
Word Family Review

Activity Directions

Word Sort (pages 42 and 43)

Students will sort words in the correct columns.

(*Extension:* Have students read the words to classmates.)

Make, Read, and Write Long Vowel Words (page 44)

Students cut out the letter and picture cards on the dashed lines. Students manipulate letter cards to form words. Students then read the words and find the matching pictures. Lastly, students may use blank paper to write the words they have formed. Use plastic baggies or envelopes to store letters and pictures.

Long Vowel Fluency Practice (page 45)

Students read the randomly placed "long a" words from left to right. Sand timers may be given to students to time how many words they can read in the given time.

My Own Long Vowel Words (page 46)

Students will write their own "long a" words on the lines provided. They can read and share their words with classmates.

(*Note:* Students can also cut on the solid lines to make flashcards.)

Making Sentences with Long A Words (page 47, 48, or 49)

Students will cut out the "long a" words and glue them in the boxes to make sentences. They can use the picture clues. Students should be encouraged to read their sentences aloud.

Word Sort

1. Cut out the **long a** words.

2. Glue each word in the correct column on the following page.

3. Be careful! There are some words that do not belong to the word families.
   Can you find them?

pain	ray	flake	play	tree
cake	ice	gray	train	brain
day	rake	seat	snake	deep
rain	say	Spain	wheat	beat
lake	chain	shake	jeep	spray

-ain	-ake	-ay

Make, Read, and Write
Long Vowel Words

Cut on the dashed lines. Make, read, and write **long a** words.

p	r	b	h	c
s	t	l	f	n
a	i	y	k	e
S	d	g		

Long Vowel Fluency Practice

Read →   Read →   Read →   Read ↑

pain	rain	brain	chain	Spain	train	cake
lake	rake	flake	shake	say	snake	day
ray	say	gray	play	spray	pain	cake
day	rain	lake	ray	brain	rake	say
chain	flake	gray	Spain	shake	play	day

My Own Long Vowel Words (long a)

46

Cut out the –**ain** words below. Glue them in the correct boxes to create sentences. Read the sentences aloud.

1. I use my  [ ] in school.

2. We rode on the [ ]  .

3. Where is 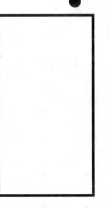 [ ] ?

4. The dog is on a  [ ] .

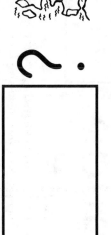

---

train	brain	Spain	chain

Making Sentences with Long A Words

Cut out the **–ake** words below. Glue them in the correct boxes to create sentences. Read the sentences aloud.

1. Let's swim in the  [ ]

2. We saw a huge  [ ]

3. Don't [ ] the can.

4. She saw a tiny  [ ]

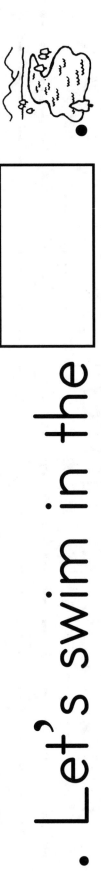

flake	lake	snake	shake

Making Sentences with Long A Words

Cut out the –ay words below. Glue them in the correct boxes to create sentences. Read the sentences aloud.

1. It is a nice  [ ] .

2. Did you see [ ]  mice ?

3. I like to [ ] jump rope.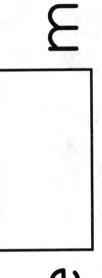

4. [ ] the sunblock on me.

---

gray   play   day   Spray

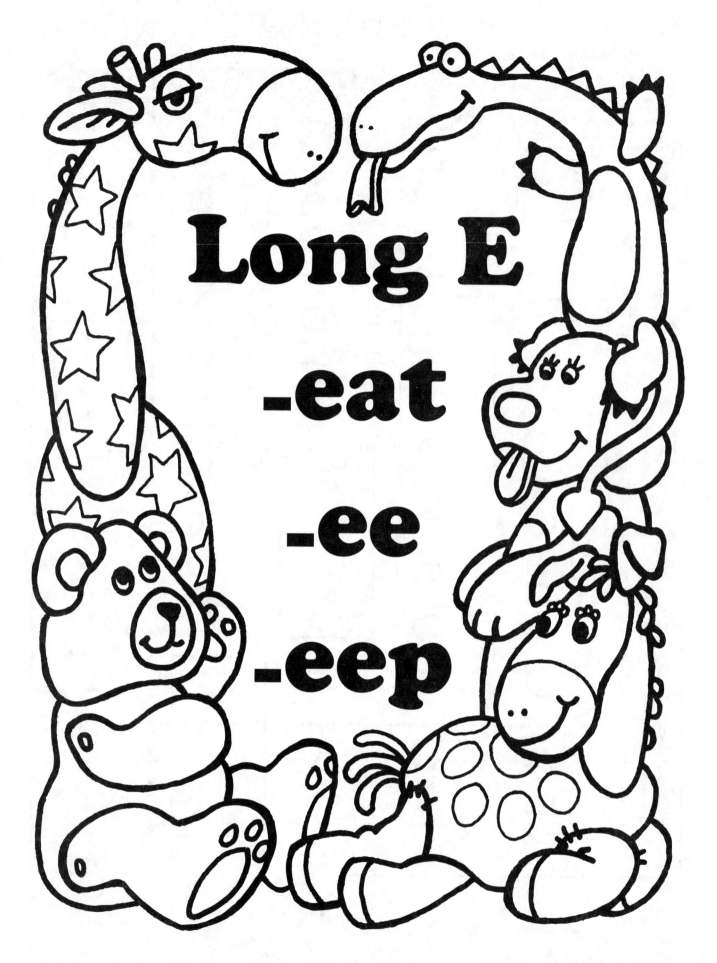

Long E
-eat
-ee
-eep

 # Part 1: Long E
Teacher Support/Home Support

Activity Directions

Letter Slide (page 52, 53, or 54)

Teacher precuts dashed lines inside pictures. Students will cut the strips of letters. Students insert the letter strips to create and manipulate "long e" words.

(Note: Students can independently ask other classmates to read the words created with the letter slide.)

Flashcards (pages 55 and 56, pages 57 and 58, or pages 59 and 60)

Copy the set of flashcards that you want the students to learn back to back (pages 55 and 56, pages 57 and 58, or pages 59 and 60). Make sure the cards align properly when copying.

Have students trace and write "long e" words on side A along with reading the words aloud. Side B will allow students to draw their own interpretations of the words. Students will then cut the cards and place then on a ring for review or use them as a reference.

Blending Boxes (page 61, 62, or 63)

First, inform students that they will be building words by listening for beginning, middle, and ending sounds. Next, the teacher stretches out the word. Both student and teacher repeat the word slowly. Then, the teacher will ask questions to help guide students to develop the sounds to write in the proper boxes. Lastly, students blend the sounds while connecting the dots to show directionality. Students read the words and practice writing them on the line.

Beginning Sound Substitution (page 64, 65, or 66)

Students cross out the beginning sounds to create new "long e" words. Use the pictures on the left as a guide. Have students read the words as they create them. Teacher must inform students that they are only substituting the beginning sounds to create new words.

Letter Slide

Cut the strip of letters. Cut the slits on the meat. Insert the strip of letters to create and manipulate the —**eat** words.

b h m s tr wh

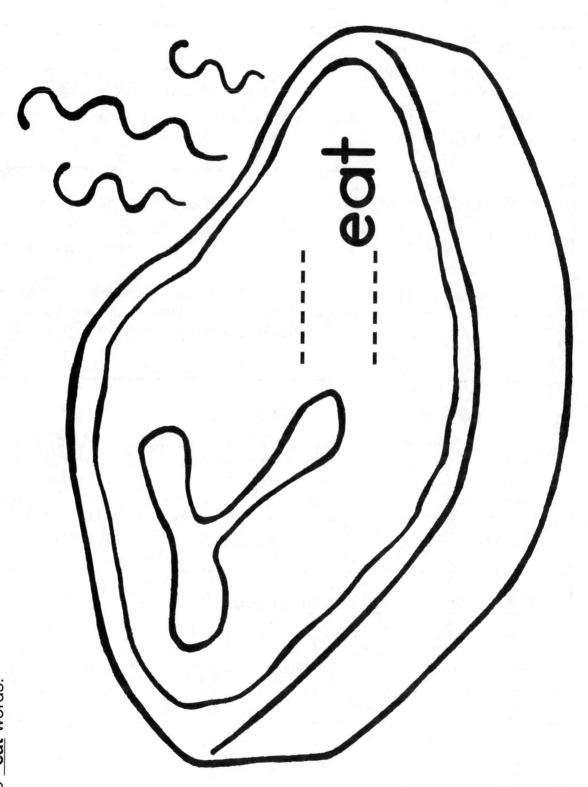

eat

Letter Slide

Cut the strip of letters. Cut the slits on the bee. Insert the strip of letters to create and manipulate the –**ee** words.

b
tr
kn
s
t
thr

ee

Letter Slide

Cut the strip of letters. Cut the slits on the jeep. Insert the strip of letters to create and manipulate the **–eep** words.

p

j

w

sl

st

sw

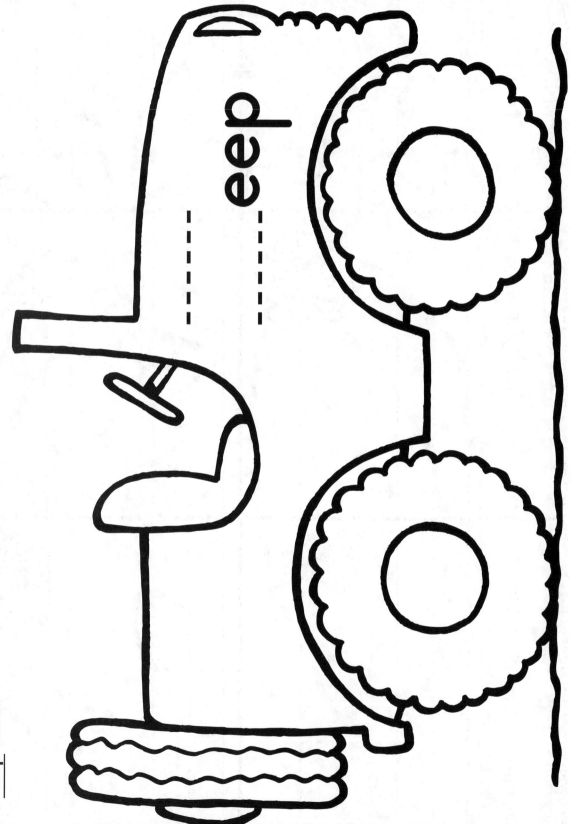

eep

seat

beat

treat

heat

wheat

meat

Side B

beat

seat

heat

treat

meat

wheat

tee

bee

tree

knee

3 three

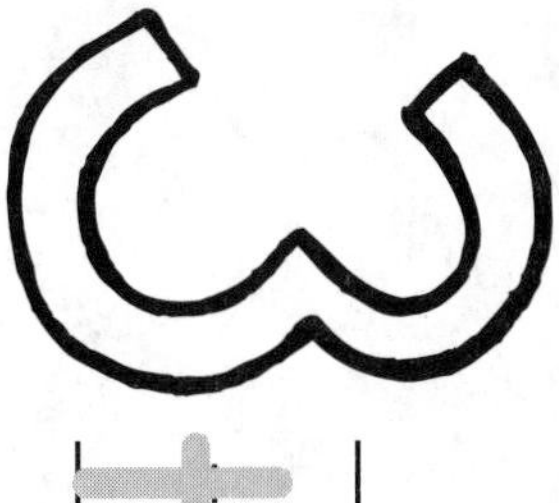

see

Side B

bee	tee
knee	tree
see	three

sleep

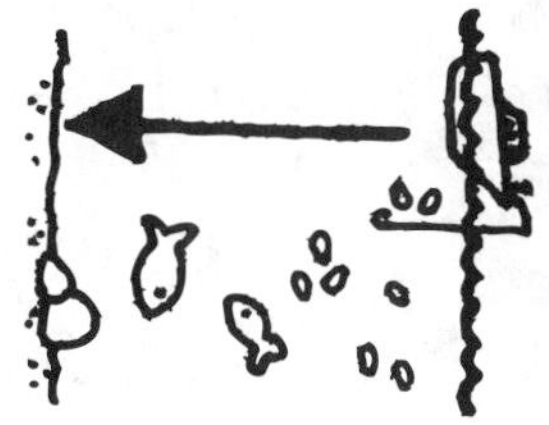

deep

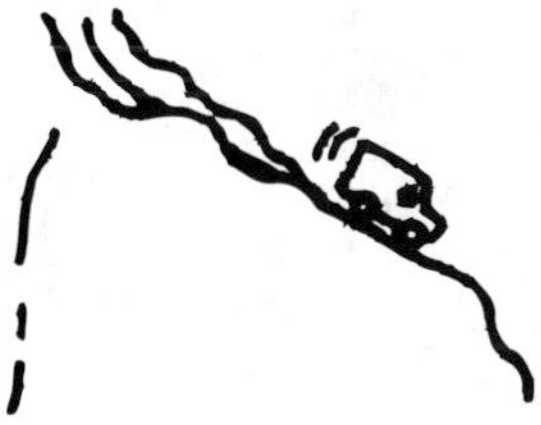

steep

jeep

sweep

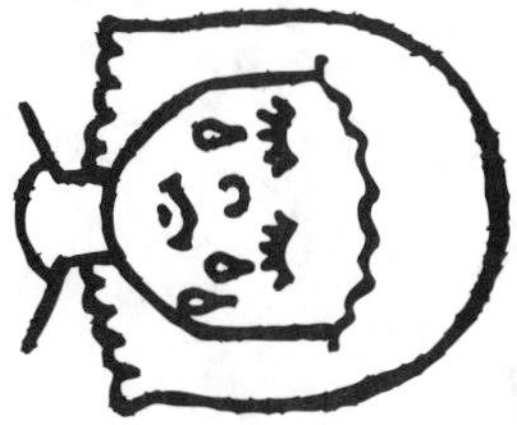

weep

deep

sleep

jeep

steep

weep

sweep

Blending Boxes

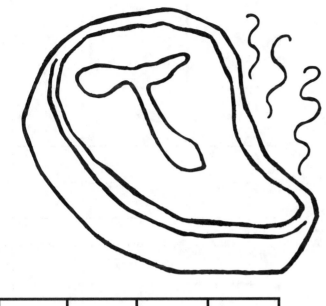

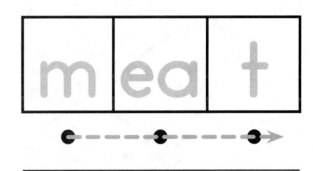

m | ea | t

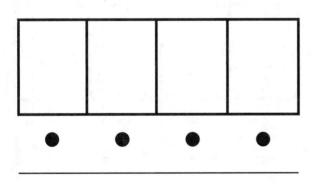

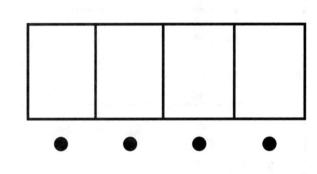

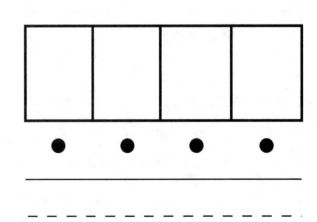

Blending Boxes

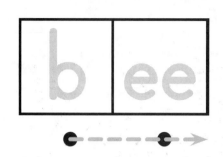

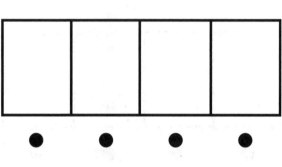

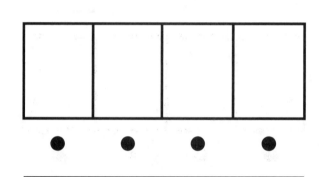

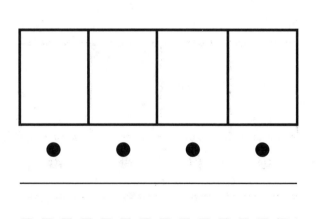

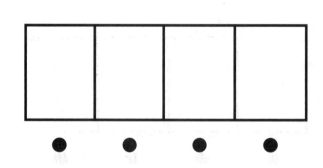

Blending Boxes

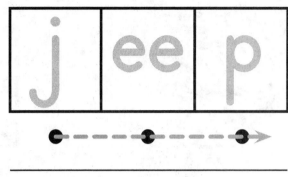

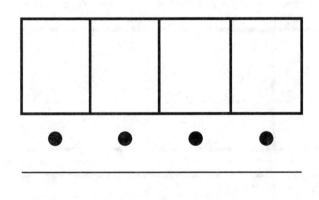

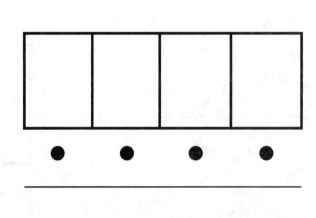

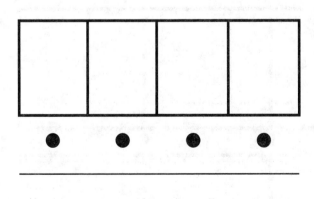

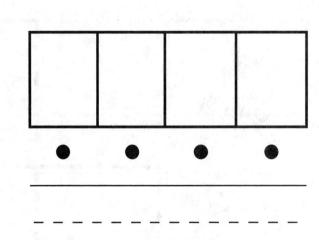

Beginning Sound Substitution

Cross out the beginning sound to create a new **–eat** word. Use the pictures on the left as a guide.

Beginning Sound Substitution

Cross out the beginning sound to create a new **–ee** word. Use the pictures on the left as a guide.

Beginning Sound Substitution

Cross out the beginning sound to create a new **–eep** word. Use the pictures on the left as a guide.

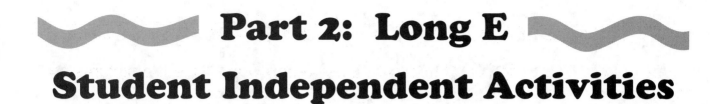

Part 2: Long E
Student Independent Activities

Activity Directions

Flip Book (pages 68–70 for *–eep*, pages 71–73 for *–ee*, pages 74–76 for *–eat*)

Copy page 2 and the "My Picture" page back to back. Make sure the dashed lines are aligned. Then copy page 1.

First, fold page 2 along the solid line and <u>only</u> cut the dashed lines.

Second, cut and glue the pictures from page 1 onto the flip book (page 2).

Third, have students draw their own pictures where it says "My Picture" in the inside.

Fourth, cut out the letter boxes from page 1. Glue letters to the corresponding pictures to make the correct words.

Fifth, have students write the words two more times.

Building Words (page 77, 78, or 79)

Cut out the letter boxes. Glue the letters in the correct boxes to create words that match the corresponding pictures.

Mystery Picture (page 80, 81, or 82)

Find and color the "long e" words to discover the mystery picture. Once the mystery picture is discovered, students will then write the "long e" mystery word in the sentence below.

Word Search (page 83, 84, or 85)

Find and color the "long e" words. Have students write the "long e" words that are found in the word search in the empty spaces below.

Flip Book (–eep)

Cut out the pictures and letters below.

Glue them on the flip book.

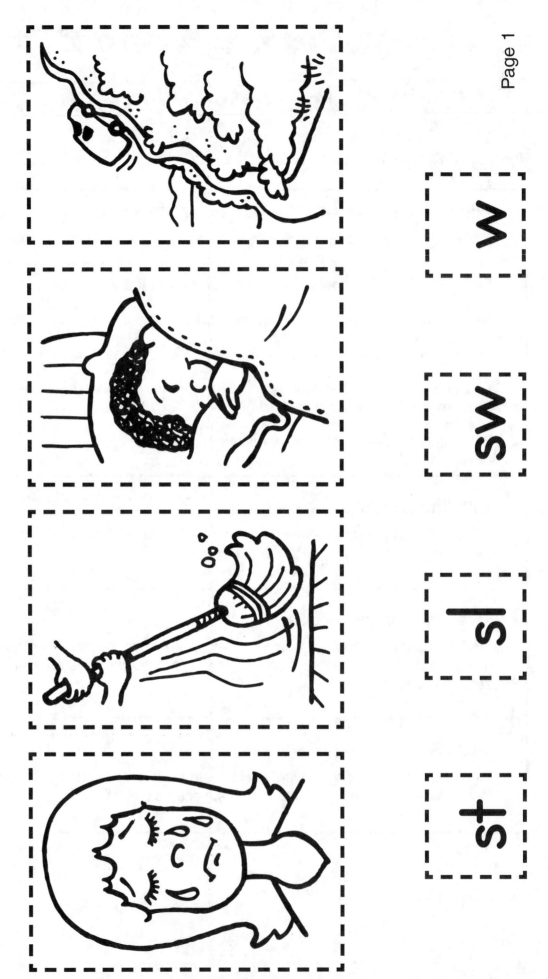

w

sw

sl

st

fold

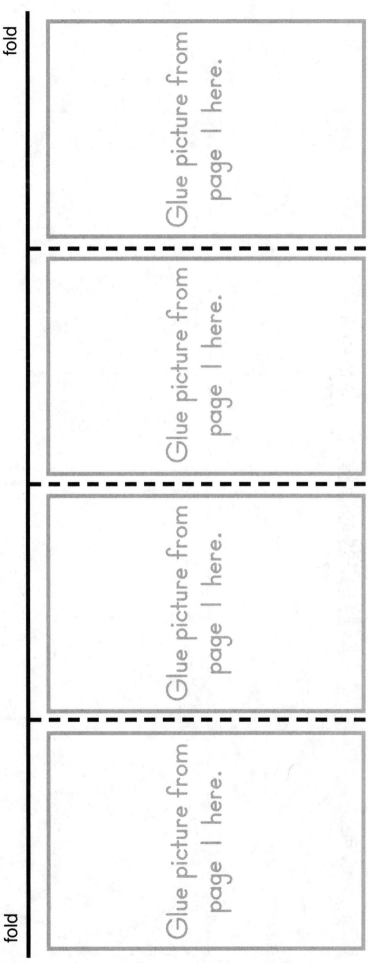

Glue picture from page 1 here.

Glue picture from page 1 here.

Glue picture from page 1 here.

Glue picture from page 1 here.

fold

My Picture		eep
My Picture		eep
My Picture		eep
My Picture		eep

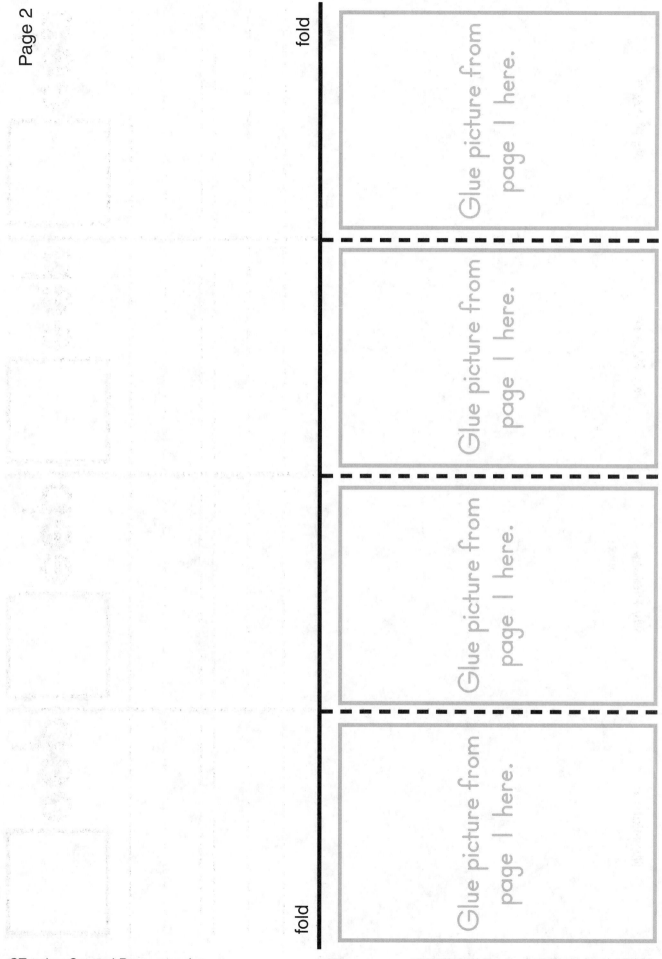

Glue picture from page 1 here.

Glue picture from page 1 here.

Glue picture from page 1 here.

Glue picture from page 1 here.

fold

fold

My Picture

My Picture

My Picture

My Picture

ee

ee

ee

ee

Flip Book (–ee)

Cut out the pictures and letters below.

Glue them on the flip book.

b

kn

tr

thr

Flip Book (–eat)

Cut out the pictures and letters below.

Glue them on the flip book.

74

Page 2

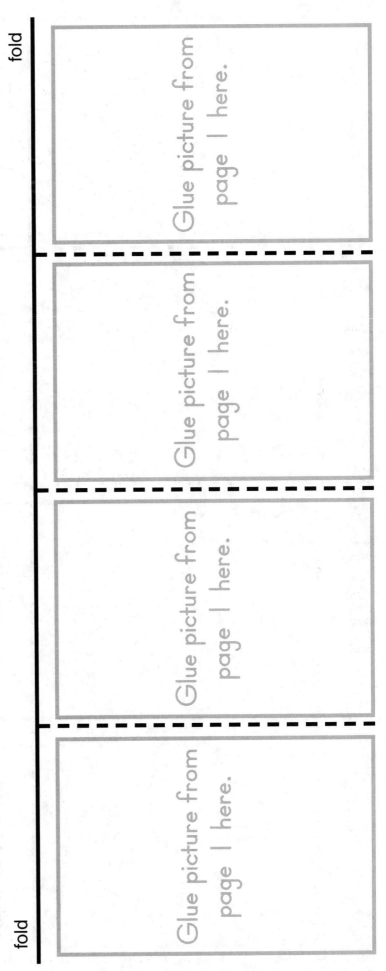

fold

Glue picture from page 1 here.

Glue picture from page 1 here.

Glue picture from page 1 here.

Glue picture from page 1 here.

fold

My Picture	eat
My Picture	eat
My Picture	eat
My Picture	eat

Building Words

Cut out the letters below. Glue them in the correct boxes to create words that match the **–eat** pictures.

Cut out the letters below. Glue them in the correct boxes to create words that match the **–ee** pictures.

b   kn   thr   tr

Building Words

Cut out the letters below. Glue them in the correct boxes to create words that match the **–eep** pictures.

eep

eep

eep

eep

st   sw   sl   w

Mystery Picture

Color the spaces with **–eat** red to discover the mystery picture. Color the other spaces yellow.

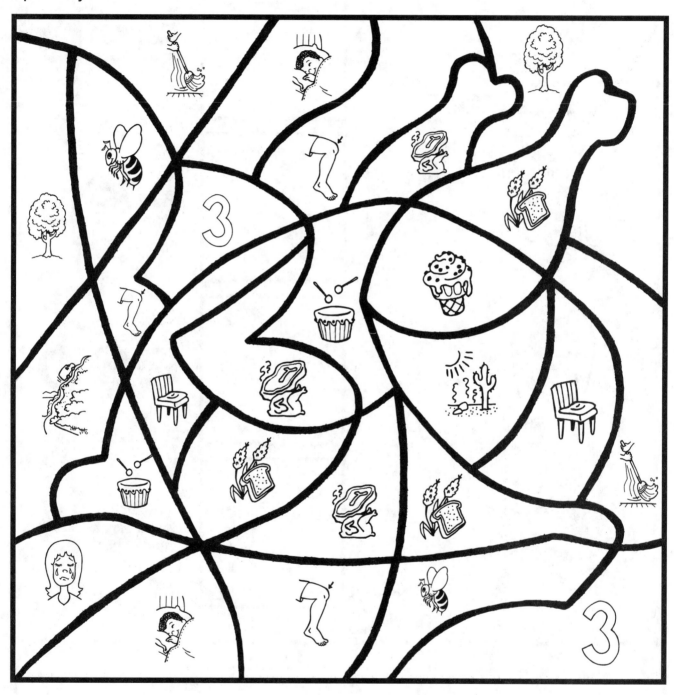

Let's eat some _____ !

Mystery Picture

Color the spaces with **–ee** blue to discover the mystery picture. Color the other spaces yellow.

We saw the number _____.

Mystery Picture

Color the spaces with **–eep** red to discover the mystery picture. Color the other spaces brown.

Help me find my _____ !

Word Search

Find and color the **–eat** words.

beat	heat	meat	seat	treat	wheat

c	b	e	a	t	d	p	h
w	h	e	a	t	m	f	e
h	a	f	n	h	t	e	a
t	r	e	a	t	i	n	t
i	n	s	k	u	u	t	n
n	e	n	b	r	a	k	n
m	e	a	t	s	e	a	t

Write the **–eat** words that you have found above.

_____   _____   _____

_____   _____   _____

_____   _____   _____

Word Search

Find and color the **–ee** words.

bee	knee	see	tee	tree	three

t	e	e	e	m	d	p	l
r	m	c	f	u	m	f	b
e	m	s	l	h	t	f	e
e	g	e	a	k	n	e	e
a	n	e	h	a	k	s	n
k	a	k	e	b	g	z	e
t	h	r	e	e	s	h	m

Write the **–ee** words that you have found above.

_____   _____   _____

_____   _____   _____

_____   _____   _____

_____   _____   _____

Word Search

Find and color the **–eep** words.

deep	jeep	weep	sleep	steep	sweep

d	s	j	e	e	p	b	t
e	m	c	w	n	l	t	e
e	s	t	e	e	p	s	d
p	e	q	e	r	t	l	g
n	t	s	p	a	u	e	r
p	l	a	p	y	g	e	w
h	f	s	w	e	e	p	y

Write the **–eep** words that you have found above.

_____   _____   _____

_____   _____   _____

Part 3: Long E
Word Family Review

Activity Directions

Word Sort (pages 87 and 88)

Students will sort words in the correct columns.

(*Extension:* Have students read the words to classmates.)

Make, Read, and Write Long Vowel Words (page 89)

Students cut out the letter and picture cards on the dashed lines. Students manipulate letter cards to form words. Students then read the words and find the matching pictures. Lastly, students may use blank paper to write the words they have formed. Use plastic baggies or envelopes to store letters and pictures.

Long Vowel Fluency Practice (page 90)

Students read the randomly placed "long e" words from left to right. Sand timers may be given to students to time how many words they can read in the given time.

My Own Long Vowel Words (page 91)

Students will write their own "long e" words on the lines provided. They can read and share their words with classmates.

(*Note:* Students can also cut on the solid lines to make flashcards.)

Making Sentences with Long E Words (page 92, 93, or 94)

Students will cut out the "long e" words and glue them in the boxes to make sentences. They can use the picture clues. Students should be encouraged to read their sentences aloud.

1. Cut out the **long e** words.

2. Glue each word in the correct column on the following page.

3. Be careful. There are some words that do not belong to the word families. Can you find them?

beat	jet	red	seat	deep
bee	hen	met	jeep	treat
knee	heat	tree	weep	three
hen	wet	tee	sleep	wheat
sweep	see	meat	get	steep

-eat	-ee	-eep

Make, Read, and Write
Long Vowel Words

Cut on the dashed lines. Make, read, and write **long e** words.

e	a	t	b	h
m	s	r	w	k
e	e	n	d	p
l	j			
3				

Long Vowel Fluency Practice

→ Read   → Read   → Read

beat   bee   deep   heat   knee   jeep   meat

see   weep   seat   tee   sleep   treat   tree

steep   wheat   three   sweep   beat   heat

meat   seat   treat   wheat   bee   knee   see

tee   tree   three   deep   jeep   weep   sleep

My Own Long Vowel Words (long e)

Making Sentences with Long E Words

Cut out the **–eat** words below. Glue them in the correct boxes to create sentences. Read the sentences aloud.

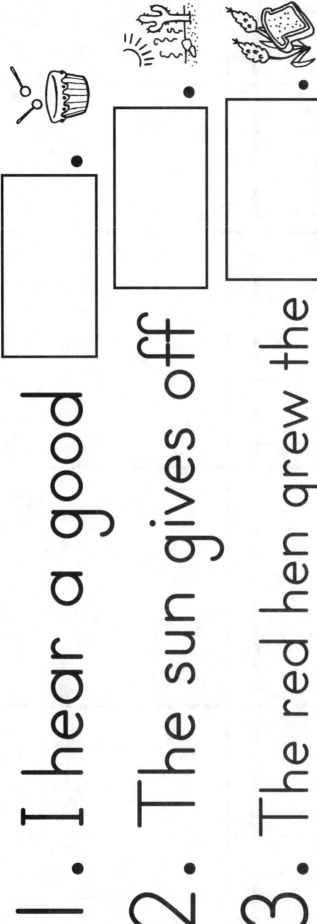

1. I hear a good

2. The sun gives off

3. The red hen grew the

4. My dog hid his

treat

heat

wheat

beat

Making Sentences with Long E Words

Cut out the _ee_ words below. Glue them in the correct boxes to create sentences. Read the sentences aloud.

1. The [ ] is yellow and black.

2. He is [ ] years old.

3. I hit the ball with my [ ].

4. I took a nap under the [ ].

---

tree	three	knee	bee

Cut out the **-eep** words below. Glue them in the correct boxes to create sentences. Read the sentences aloud.

1. Can we go to [   ] ?

2. Where is my green [   ] ?

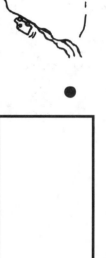

3. I need to [   ] the floor.

4. The hill is very [   ].

| steep | sleep | jeep | sweep |

Long I
-ice
-ight
-ine

Part 1: Long I
Teacher Support/Home Support

Activity Directions

Flashcards (pages 97 and 98, pages 99 and 100, or pages 101 and 102)

Copy the set of flashcards that you want the students to learn back to back (pages 97 and 98, pages 99 and 100, or pages 101 and 102). Make sure the cards align properly when copying.

Have students trace and rewrite "long i" words on side A along with reading the words aloud. Side B will allow students to draw their own interpretations of the words. Students will then cut out the cards and place them on a ring for review or use them as a reference.

Letter Slide (page 103, 104, or 105)

Teacher precuts dashed lines inside picture. Students will cut the strips of letters. Students insert the letter strips to create and manipulate "long i" words.

(*Note:* Students can independently ask other classmates to read the words created with the letter slide.)

Blending Boxes (page 106, 107, or 108)

First, inform students that they will be building words by listening for beginning, middle, and ending sounds. Next, the teacher stretches out the word. Both student and teacher repeat the word slowly. Then, the teacher will ask questions to help guide students to develop the sounds to write in the proper boxes. Lastly, students blend the sounds while connecting the dots to show directionality. Students read the words and practice writing them on the line.

Beginning Sound Substitution (page 109, 110, or 111)

Students cross out the beginning sound to create a new "long i" word. Use the pictures on the left as a guide. Have students read the words as they create them. Teacher must inform students that they are only substituting the beginning sound to create new words.

rice

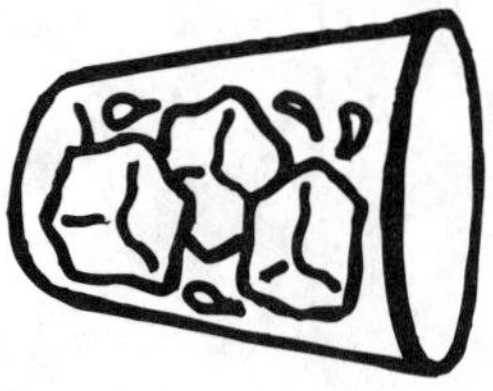

ice

price

dice

slice

mice

Side B

ice

rice

dice

price

mice

slice

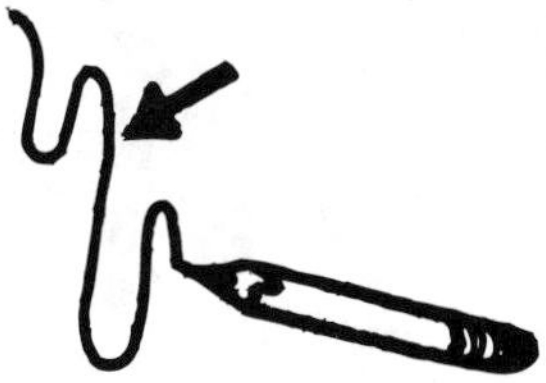

vine

line

shine

nine

spine

pine

Side B

line	vine
nine	shine
pine	spine

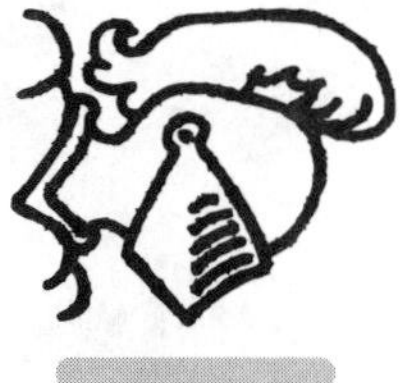

right

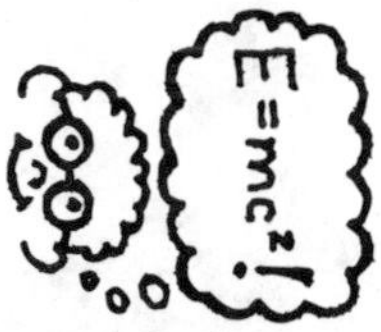

knight

bright

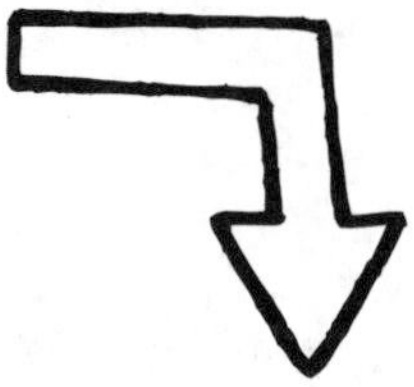

light

flight

night

knight

right

light

bright

night

flight

Letter Slide

Cut the strip of letters. Cut the slits on the dice. Insert the strip of letters to create and manipulate the **–ice** words.

d m r pr sl

_ _ _ ice

Letter Slide

Cut the strip of letters. Cut the slits on the light bulb. Insert the strip of letters to create and manipulate the **–ight** words.

_ _ _ _ _ _ _ight

kn
l
n
br
fl
r

Letter Slide

Cut the strip of letters. Cut the slits on the pine tree. Insert the strip of letters to create and manipulate the **–ine** words.

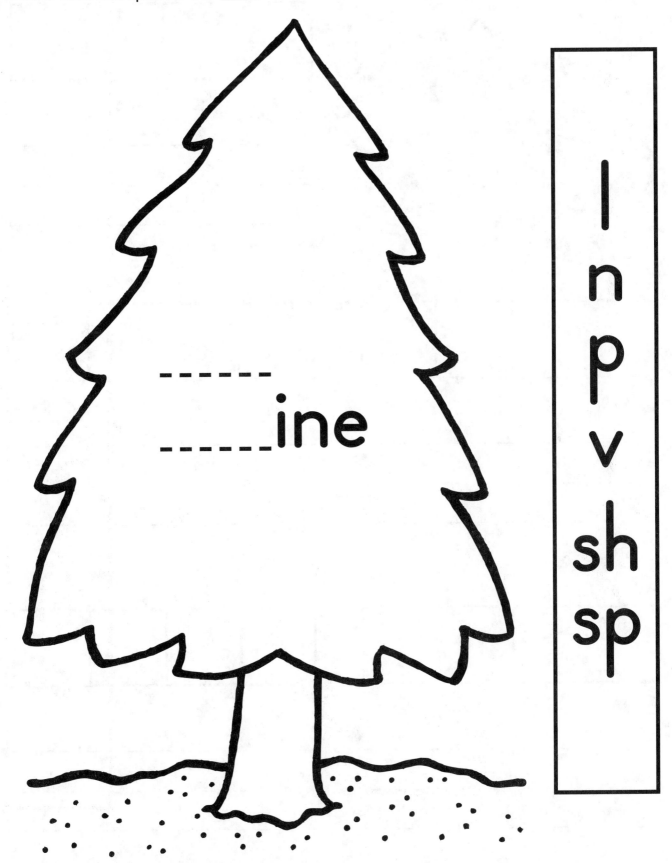

_____ine

l
n
p
v
sh
sp

Blending Boxes

Blending Boxes

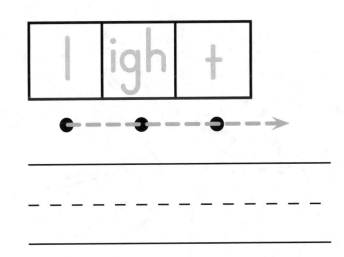

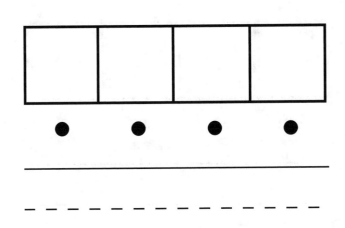

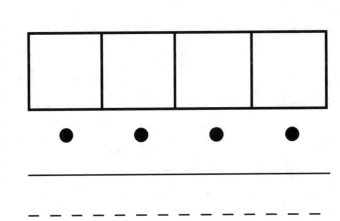

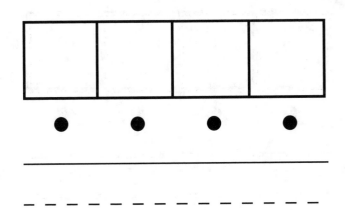

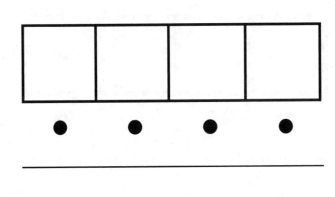

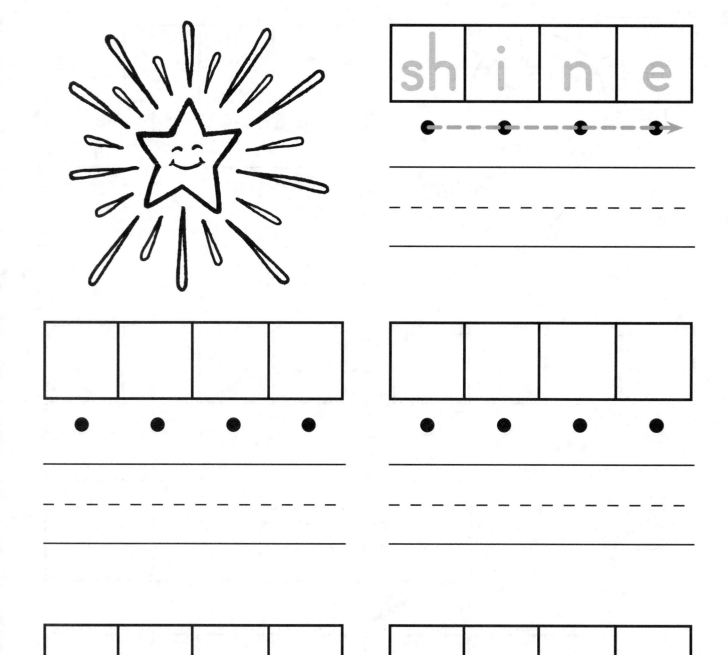

Beginning Sound Substitution

Add a beginning sound to create a new **–ice** word. Use the pictures on the left as a guide.

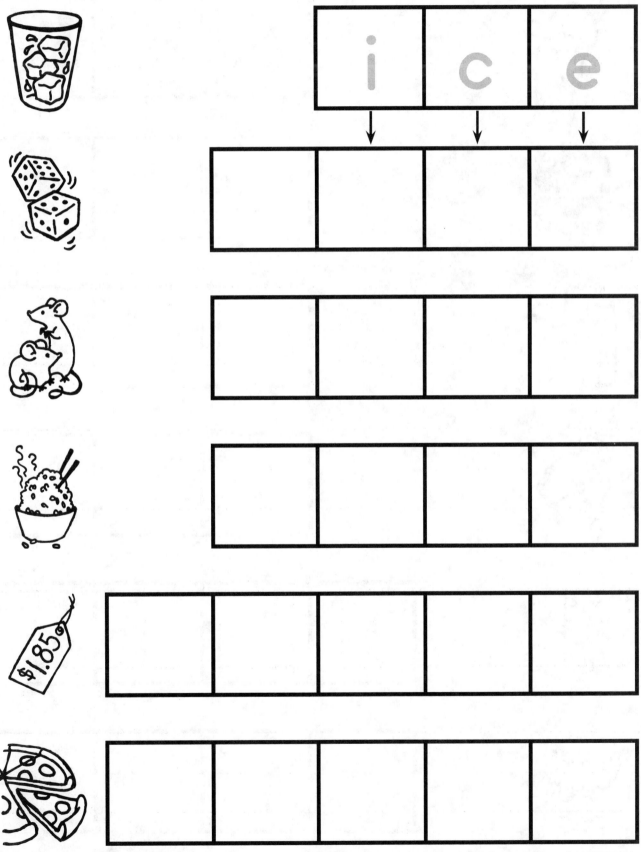

Beginning Sound Substitution

Cross out the beginning sound to create a new **–ight** word. Use the pictures on the left as a guide.

Beginning Sound Substitution

Cross out the beginning sound to create a new **–ine** word. Use the pictures on the left as a guide.

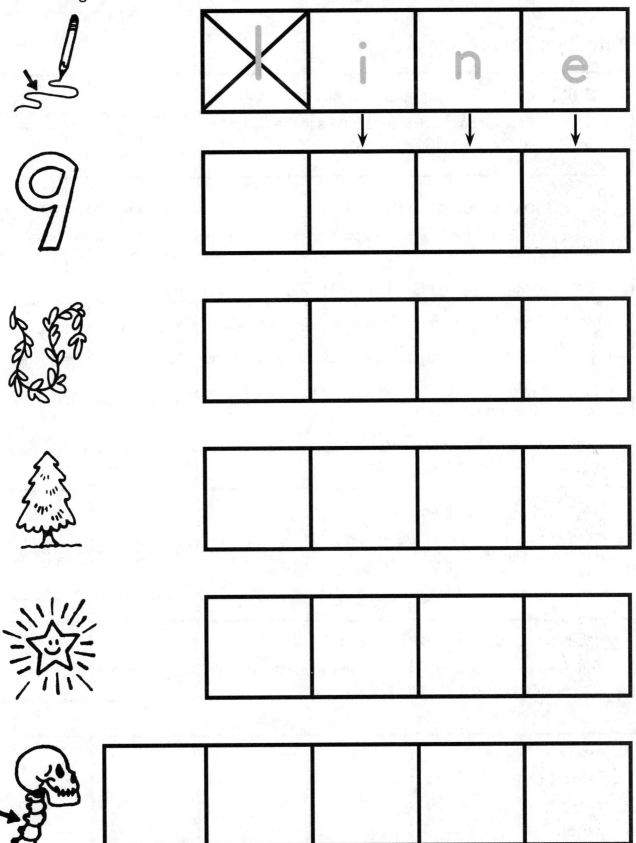

Part 2: Long I
Student Independent Activities

Activity Directions

Building Words (page 113, 114, or 115)

Cut out the letter boxes. Glue the letters in the correct boxes to create words that match the corresponding pictures.

Flip Book (pages 116 –118 for *–ice*, pages 119–121 *–ight,* or pages 122–124 for *–ine*)

Copy page 2 and the "My Picture" page back to back. Make sure the dashed lines are aligned. Then copy page 1.

First, fold page 2 along the solid line and only cut the dashed lines.

Second, cut and glue the pictures from page 1 onto the flip book (page 2).

Third, have students draw their own pictures where it says, "My Picture" in the inside.

Fourth, cut out the letter boxes from page 1. Glue letters to the corresponding pictures to make the correct words.

Fifth, have students write the words two more times.

Mystery Picture (page 125, 126, or 127)

Find and color the "long i" words to discover the mystery picture. Once the mystery picture is discovered, students will then write the "long i" mystery word in the sentence below.

Word Search (page 128, 129, or 130)

Find and color the "long i" words. Have students write the "long i" words that are found in the word search in the empty spaces below.

Cut out the letters below. Glue them in the correct boxes to create words that match the **–ice** pictures.

Building Words

Cut out the letters below. Glue them in the correct boxes to create words that match the **–ight** pictures.

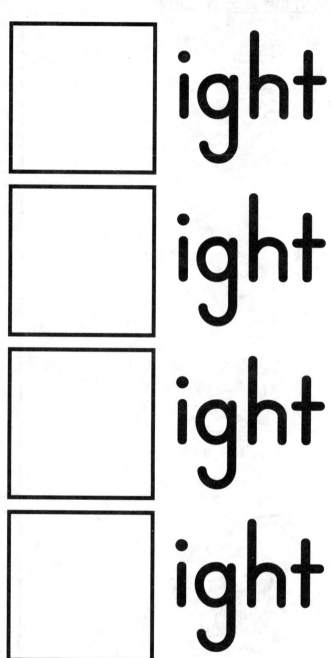

☐ ight

☐ ight

☐ ight

☐ ight

- -

| br | fl | l | kn |

Building Words

Cut out the letters below. Glue them in the correct boxes to create words that match the **–ine** pictures.

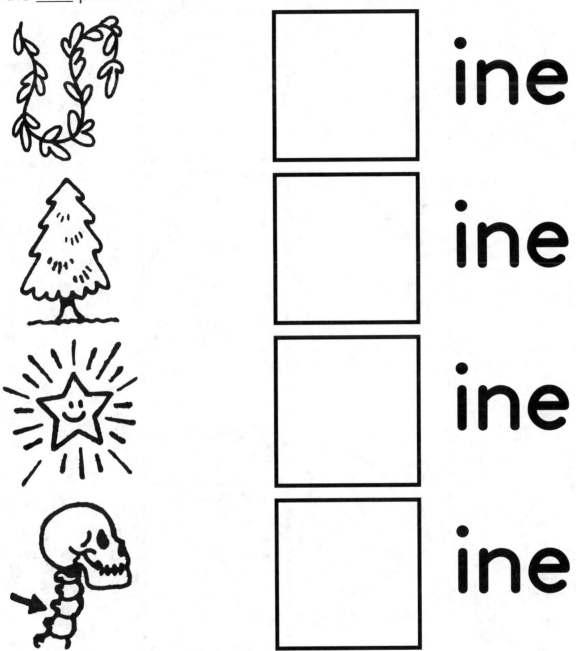

	ine
	ine
	ine
	ine

sh	sp	v	p

Flip Book (-ice)

Cut out the pictures and letters below.

Glue them on the flip book.

p

m

pr

sl

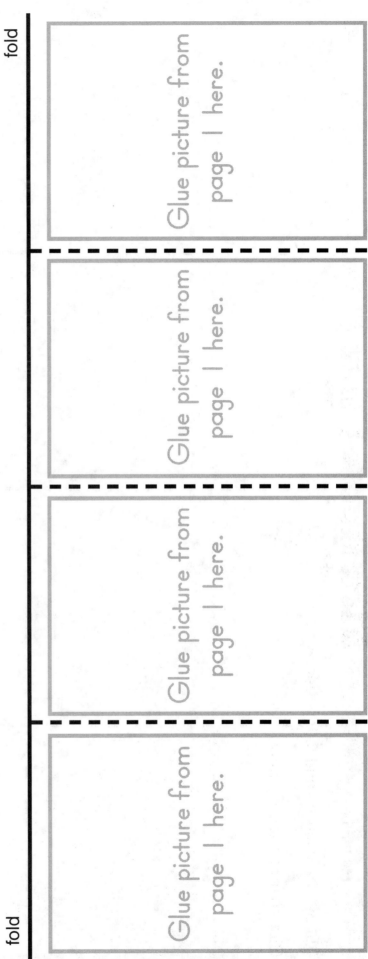

fold

fold

Glue picture from page 1 here.

Glue picture from page 1 here.

Glue picture from page 1 here.

Glue picture from page 1 here.

My Picture

My Picture

My Picture

My Picture

ice

ice

ice

ice

118

fold

Glue picture from page 1 here.

Glue picture from page 1 here.

Glue picture from page 1 here.

Glue picture from page 1 here.

fold

My Picture

My Picture

My Picture

My Picture

ight

ight

ight

ight

Flip Book (–ight)

Cut out the pictures and letters below.

Glue them on the flip book.

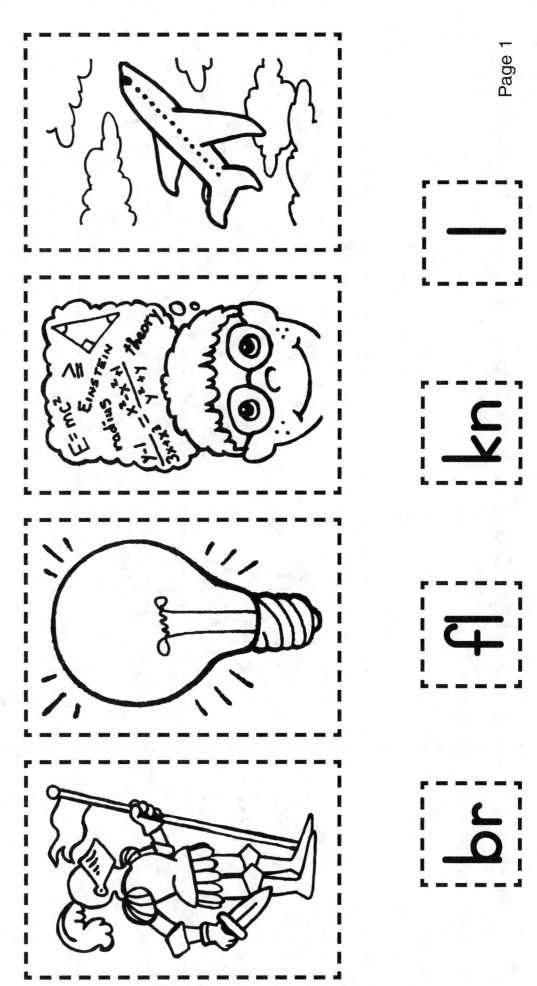

121

Flip Book (–ine)

Cut out the pictures and letters below.

Glue them on the flip book.

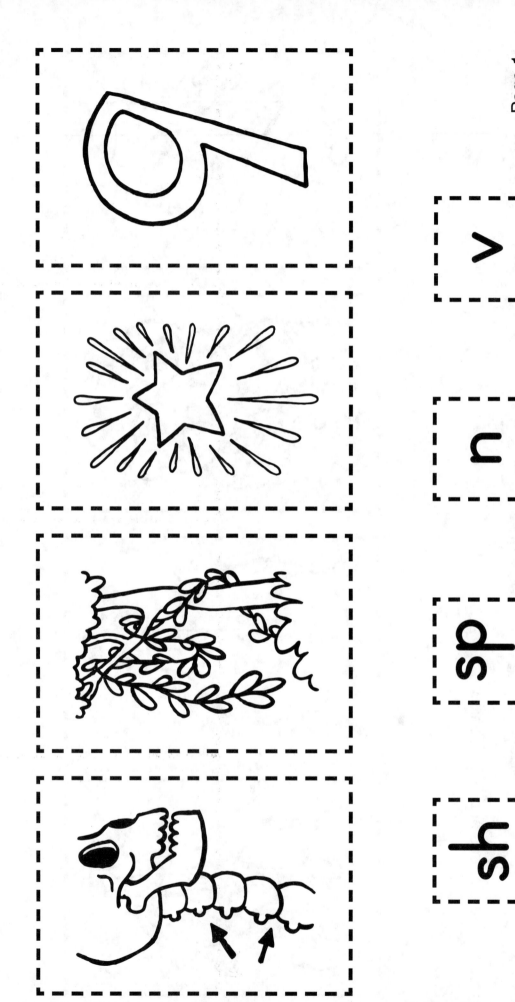

v

n

sp

sh

Page 2

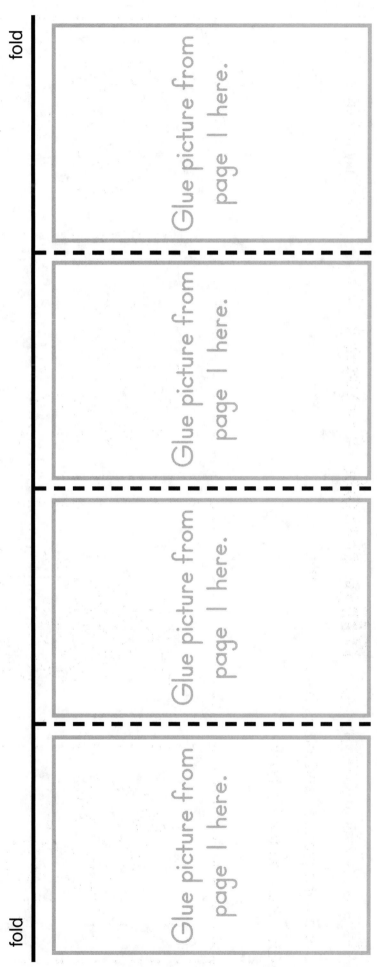

fold

Glue picture from
page 1 here.

Glue picture from
page 1 here.

Glue picture from
page 1 here.

Glue picture from
page 1 here.

fold

My Picture

My Picture

My Picture

My Picture

_ine

_ine

_ine

_ine

Mystery Picture

Color the spaces with **–ice** gray to discover the mystery picture. Color the other spaces green.

The _____ are gray !

Color the spaces with **–ight** yellow to discover the mystery picture. Color the other spaces gray.

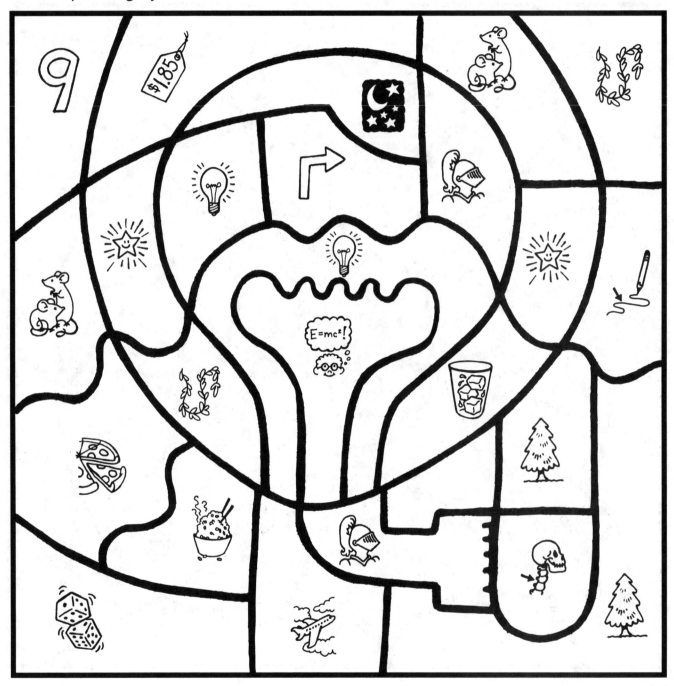

I turned on the _____ !

Mystery Picture

Color the spaces with **–ine** yellow to discover the mystery picture. Color the other spaces black.

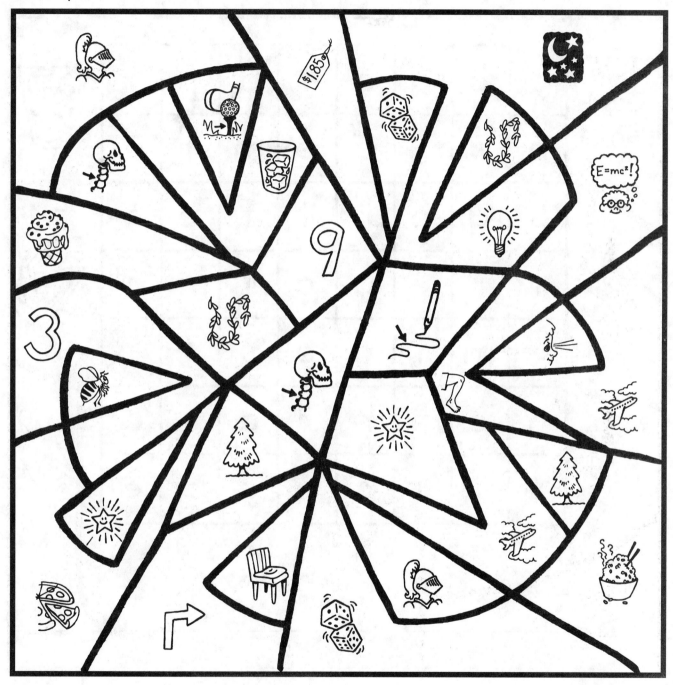

Could you see the star _____ ?

 # Word Search

Find and color the **–ice** words.

dice	mice	rice	price	slice	ice

c	b	d	a	t	d	p	i
p	r	i	c	e	m	f	c
h	a	c	n	i	t	e	e
t	r	e	a	c	i	n	r
i	m	i	c	e	u	t	i
n	e	n	b	r	a	i	c
s	l	i	c	e	d	a	e

Write the **–ice** words that you have found above.

_____ _____ _____

_____ _____ _____

_____ _____ _____

_____ _____ _____

Word Search

Find and color the **–ight** words.

| knight | light | night | right | bright | flight |

t	k	n	i	g	h	t	l
r	b	r	i	g	h	t	n
i	m	f	l	h	i	e	i
g	e	q	a	k	g	e	g
h	n	s	h	a	h	e	h
t	l	i	g	h	t	z	t
f	l	i	g	h	t	e	e

Write the **–ight** words that you have found above.

_____   _____   _____

_____   _____   _____

_____   _____   _____

_____   _____   _____

Word Search

Find and color the **–ine** words.

line	nine	pine	vine	shine	spine

l	s	p	i	n	e	e	t
i	m	c	p	n	e	t	e
n	s	t	i	e	p	s	s
e	e	q	n	r	t	l	h
n	i	n	e	a	u	e	i
p	l	a	p	y	g	e	n
h	f	s	v	i	n	e	e

Write the **–ine** words that you have found above.

_____   _____   _____

_____   _____   _____

_____   _____   _____

Part 3: Long I
Word Family Review

Activity Directions

Word Sort (pages 132 and 133)

Students will sort words in the correct columns.

(*Extension:* Have students read the words to classmates.)

Make, Read, and Write Long Vowel Words (page 134)

Students cut out the letter and picture cards on the dashed lines. Students manipulate letter cards to form words. Students then read the words and find the matching pictures. Lastly, students may use blank paper to write the words they found. Use plastic baggies or envelopes to store letters and pictures.

Long Vowel Fluency Practice (page 135)

Students read the randomly placed "long i" words from left to right. Sand timers may be given to students to time how many words they can read in the given time.

My Own Long Vowel Words (page 136)

Students will write their own "long i" words on the lines provided. They can read and share their words with classmates.

(*Note:* Students can also cut on the solid lines to make flashcards.)

Making Sentences with Long I Words (page 137, 138, or 139)

Students will cut out the "long i" words and glue them in the boxes to make sentences. They can use the picture clues. Students should be encouraged to read their sentences aloud.

Word Sort

1. Cut out the **long i** words.

2. Glue each word in the correct column on the following page.

3. Be careful. There are some words that do not belong to the word families. Can you find them?

slice	chin	mice	rice	shine
light	knight	kid	price	line
spine	zip	nine	night	ice
dice	big	twig	right	bright
vine	flight	pit	flip	pine

-ice	-ight	-ine

Make, Read, and Write
Long Vowel Words

Cut on the dashed lines. Make, read, and write **long i** words.

i	g	h	t	k
n	n	r	b	f
l	e	p	v	sh
s	d	c	m	☆

Read → Read → Read →

dice	mice	rice	price	slice	ice	knight
night	right	bright	flight	line	nine	vine
shine	spine	dice	knight	line	mice	light
rice	night	pine	price	bright	vine	slice
right	shine	ice	flight	spine	dice	light

My Own Long Vowel Words (long i)

Making Sentences with Long I Words

Cut out the –ice words below. Glue them in the correct boxes to create sentences. Read the sentences aloud.

1. I enjoy eating 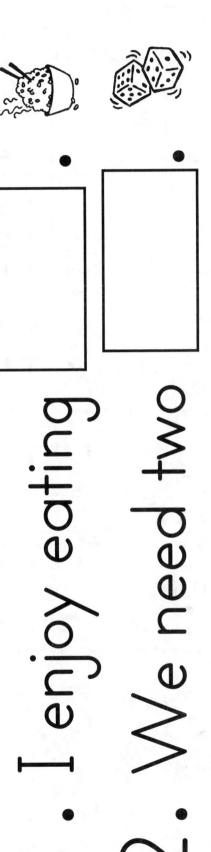 .

2. We need two  .

3. I want a 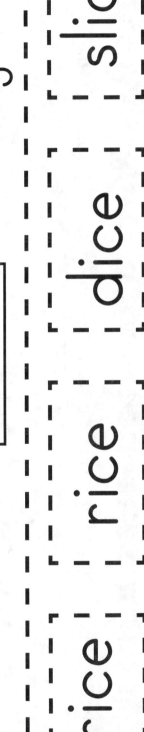 of pizza.

4. Tell me the  of this game.

| price | rice | dice | slice |

Making Sentences with Long I Words

Cut out the **–ight** words below. Glue them in the correct boxes to create sentences. Read the sentences aloud.

1. Turn off the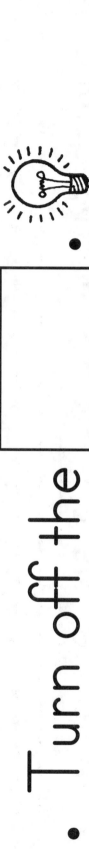

2. The [ ] lives far away.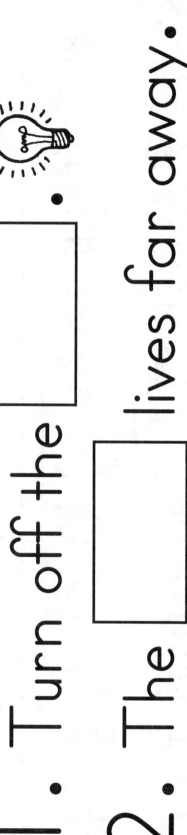

3. My friend is very [ ]

4. Last week we took a [ ]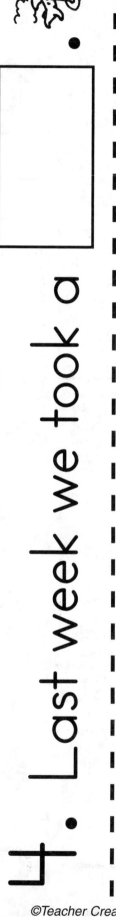

flight   light   knight   bright

Making Sentences with Long I Words

Cut out the **-ine** words below. Glue them in the correct boxes to create sentences. Read the sentences aloud.

1. The [ ] grew long.

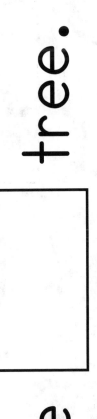

2. I smell the [ ] tree.

3. I need to [ ] the floor.

4. My [ ] is hurting.

vine | pine | shine | spine

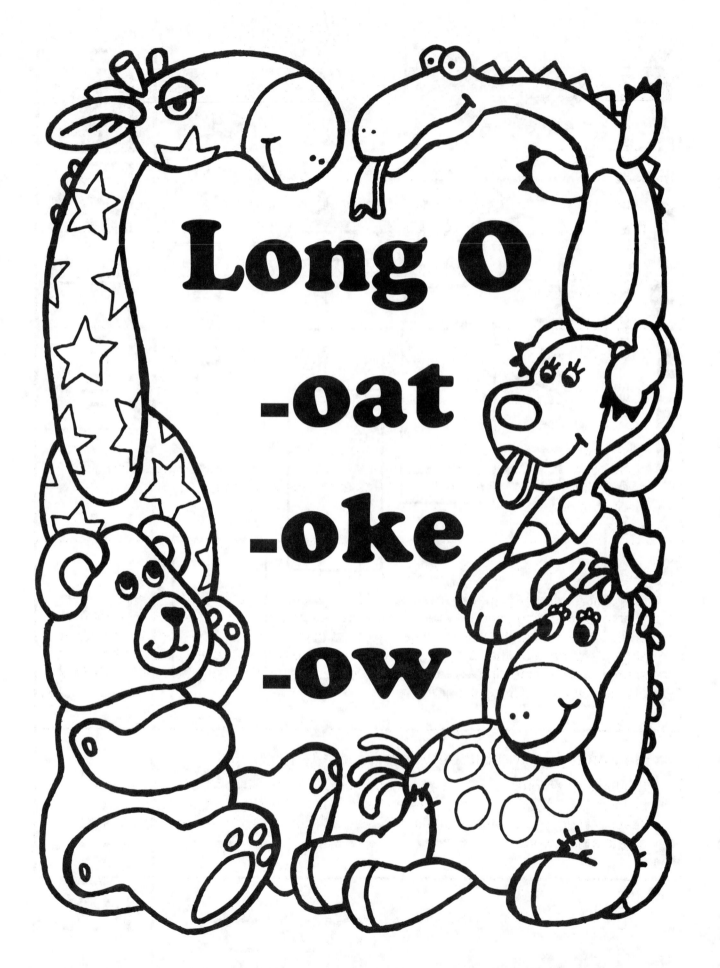

Long O

-oat

-oke

-ow

Part 1: Long O
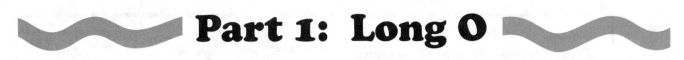
Teacher Support/Home Support

Activity Directions

Letter Slide (page 142, 143, or 144)

Teacher precuts dashed lines inside pictures. Students will cut the strips of letters. Students insert the letter strips to create and manipulate "long o" words.

(*Note:* Students can independently ask other classmates to read the words created with the letter slide.)

Flashcards (pages 145 and 146, pages 147 and 148, or pages 149 and 150)

Copy the set of flashcards that you want the students to learn back to back (pages 145 and 146, pages 147 and 148, or pages 149 and 150). Make sure the cards align properly when copying.

Have students trace and rewrite "long o" words on side A along with reading the words aloud. Side B will allow students to draw their own interpretations of the words once again. Students will then cut out the cards and place them on a ring for review or use them as a reference.

Blending Boxes (page 151, 152, or 153)

First, inform students that they will be building words by listening for beginning, middle, and ending sounds. Next, the teacher stretches out the word. Both student and teacher repeat the word slowly. Then, the teacher will ask questions to help guide students to develop the sounds to write in the proper boxes. Lastly, students blend the sounds while connecting the dots to show directionality. Students read the words and practice writing them on the line.

Beginning Sound Substitution (page 154, 155, or 156)

Students cross out the beginning sound to create a new "long o" word. Use the pictures on the left as a guide. Have students read the words as they create them. Teacher must inform students that they are only substituting the beginning sound to create a new word.

Letter Slide

Cut the strip of letters. Cut the slits on the goat. Insert the strip of letters to create and manipulate the **–oat** words.

b
c
g
gl
fl
thr

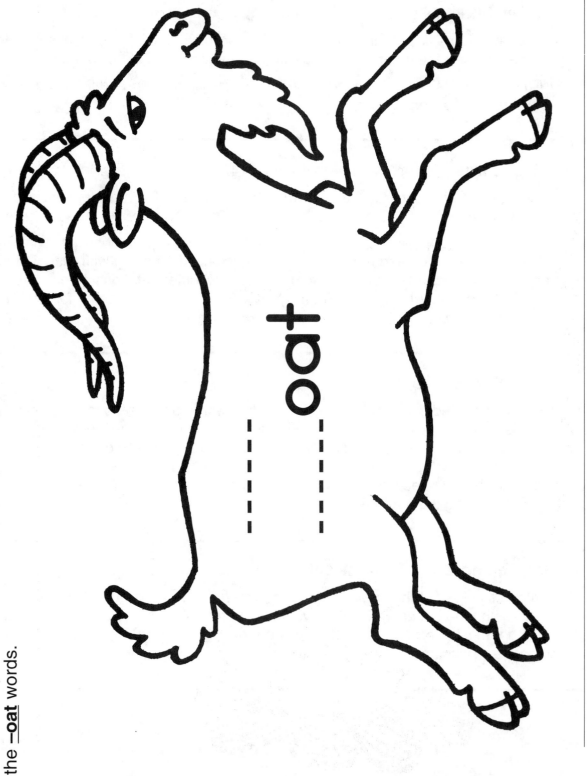

oat

Letter Slide

Cut the strip of letters. Cut the slits on the smoke. Insert the strip of letters to create and manipulate the **–oke** words.

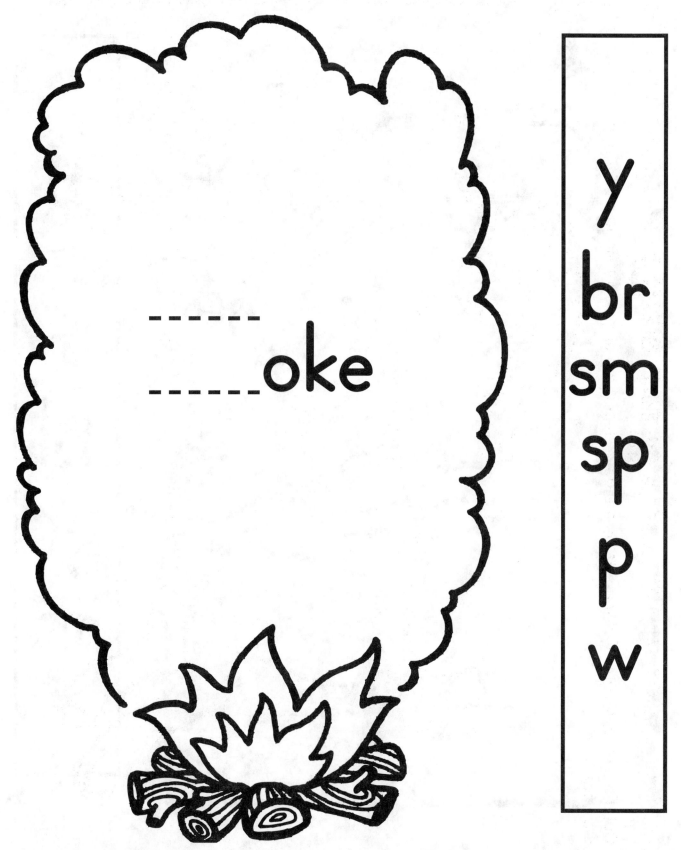

_____

_____oke

y
br
sm
sp
p
w

Letter Slide

Cut the strip of letters. Cut the slits on the snow. Insert the strip of letters to create and manipulate the **–ow** words.

_____

_____ow

b
r
t
bl
gr
sn

gloat

I did better than everybody.

boat

float

coat

throat

goat

Side B

boat

gloat

coat

float

goat

throat

broke

poke

smoke

woke

spoke

yoke

Side B

poke

broke

woke

smoke

yoke

spoke

blow

bow

grow

row

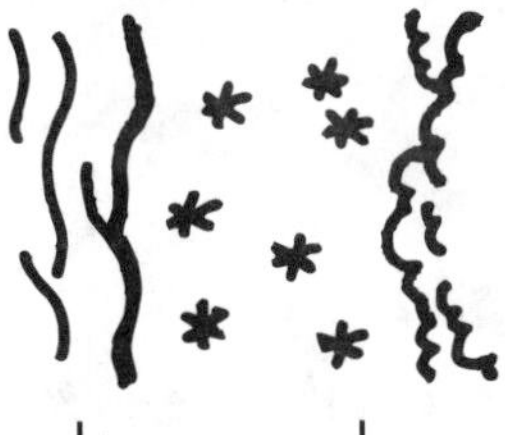

snow

tow

bow

blow

row

grow

tow

snow

Blending Boxes

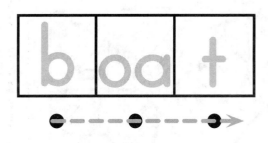

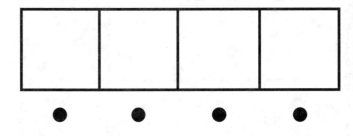

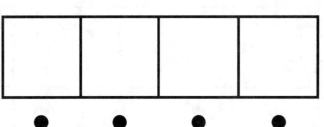

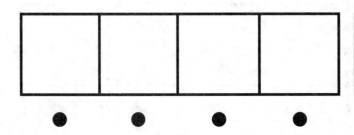

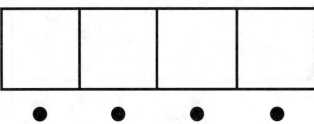

Blending Boxes

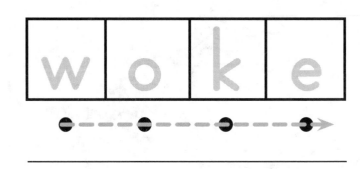

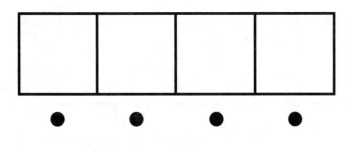

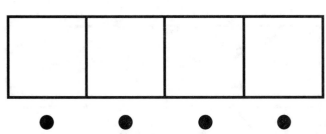 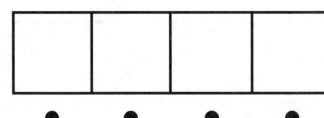

Blending Boxes

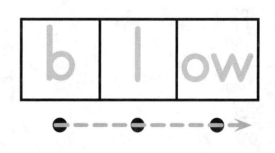

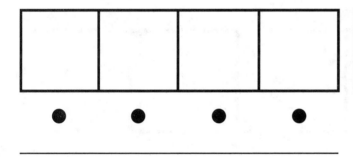

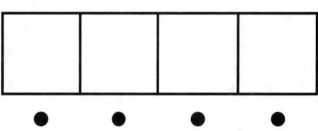

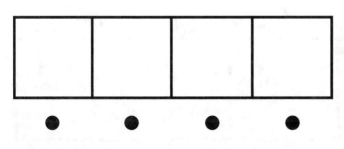

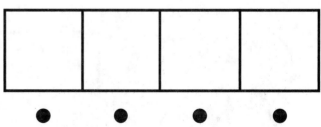

Beginning Sound Substitution

Cross out the beginning sound to create a new **–oat** word. Use the pictures on the left as a guide.

Beginning Sound Substitution

Cross out the beginning sound to create a new **–oke** word. Use the pictures on the left as a guide.

Beginning Sound Substitution

Cross out the beginning sound to create a new **–ow** word. Use the pictures on the left as a guide.

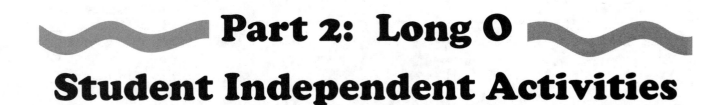

Part 2: Long O
Student Independent Activities

Activity Directions

Flip Book (pages 158–160 for *–oat*, pages 161–163 for *–oke*, or pages 164–166 for *–ow*)

Copy page 2 and the "My Picture" page back to back. Make sure the dashed lines are aligned. Then copy page 1.

First, fold page 2 along the solid line and only cut the dashed lines.

Second, cut and glue the pictures from page 1 onto the flip book (page 2).

Third, have students draw their own pictures where it says "My Picture" in the inside.

Fourth, cut out the letter boxes from page 1. Glue letters to the corresponding pictures to make the correct words.

Fifth, have students write the words two more times.

Building Words (page 167, 168, or 169)

Cut out the letter boxes. Glue the letters in the correct boxes to create words that match the corresponding pictures.

Mystery Picture (page 170, 171, or 172)

Find and color the "long o" words to discover the mystery picture. Once the mystery picture is discovered, students will then write the "long o" mystery word in the sentence below.

Word Search (page 173, 174, or 175)

Find and color the "long o" words. Have students write the "long o" words that are found in the word search in the empty spaces below.

Flip Book (–oat)

Cut out the pictures and letters below.

Glue them on the flip book.

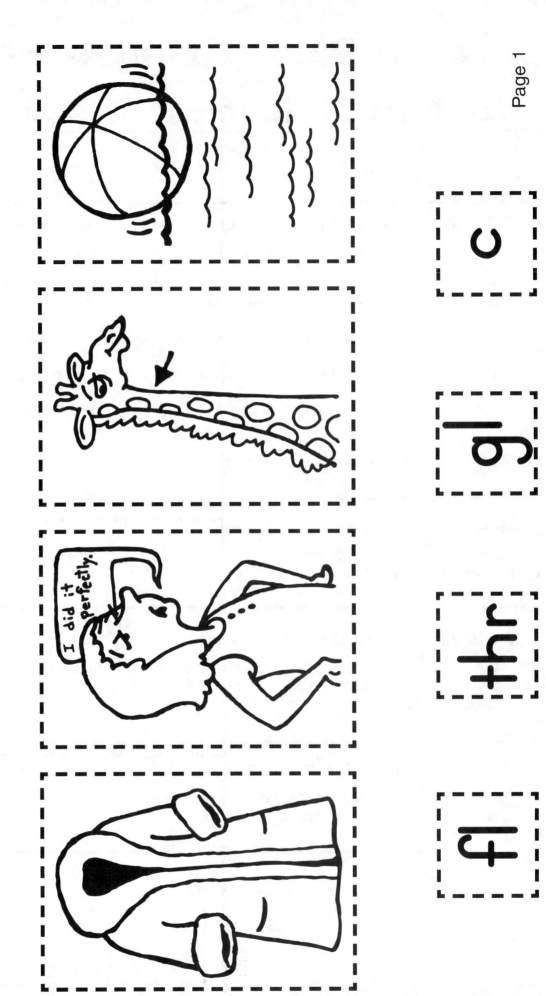

158

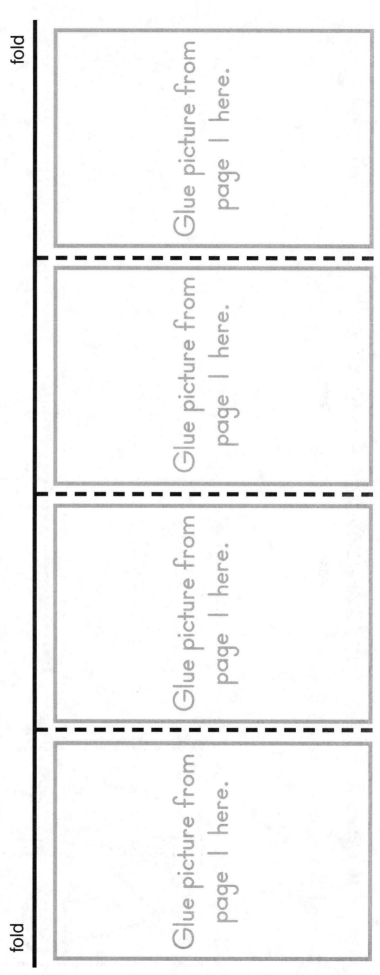

My Picture

My Picture

My Picture

My Picture

oat

oat

oat

oat

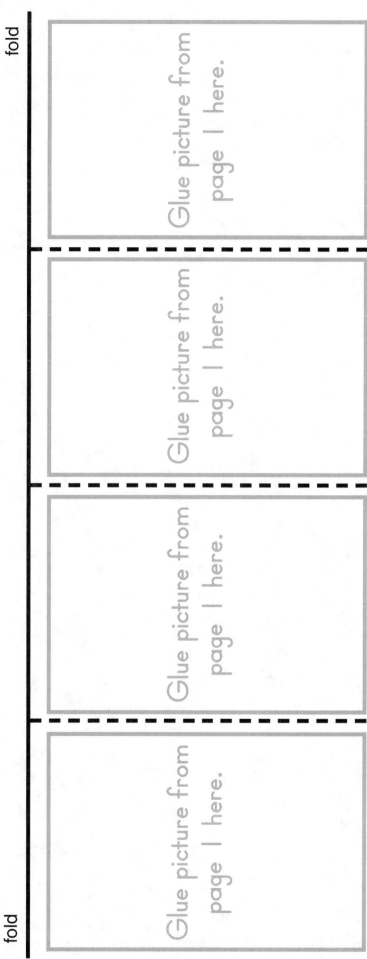

My Picture

My Picture

My Picture

My Picture

oke

oke

oke

oke

Flip Book (–oke)

Cut out the pictures and letters below.

Glue them on the flip book.

y

br

sp

sm

Flip Book (-ow)

Cut out the pictures and letters below.

Glue them on the flip book.

t

bl

gr

sn

fold

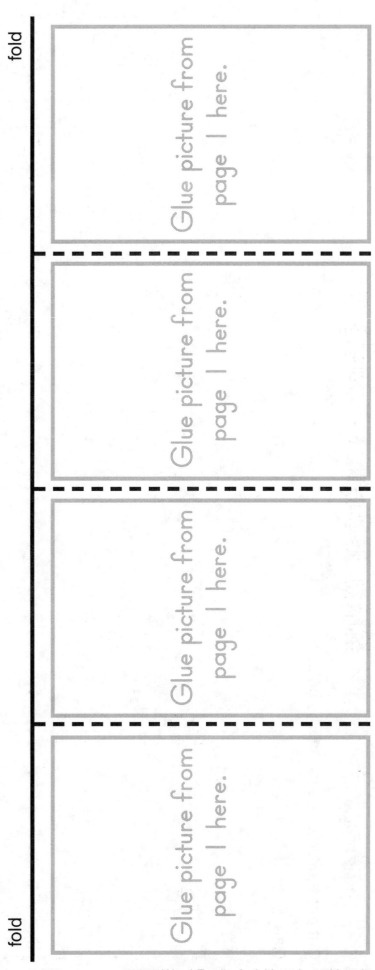

fold

My Picture

My Picture

My Picture

My Picture

ow

ow

ow

ow

Building Words

Cut out the letters below. Glue them in the correct boxes to create words that match the **–oat** pictures.

 oat

 oat

 oat

 oat

gl   fl   thr   b

Building Words

Cut out the letters below. Glue them in the correct boxes to create words that match the **–oke** pictures.

oke

oke

oke

oke

sp   sm   br   y

168

Building Words

Cut out the letters below. Glue them in the correct boxes to create words that match the **–ow** pictures.

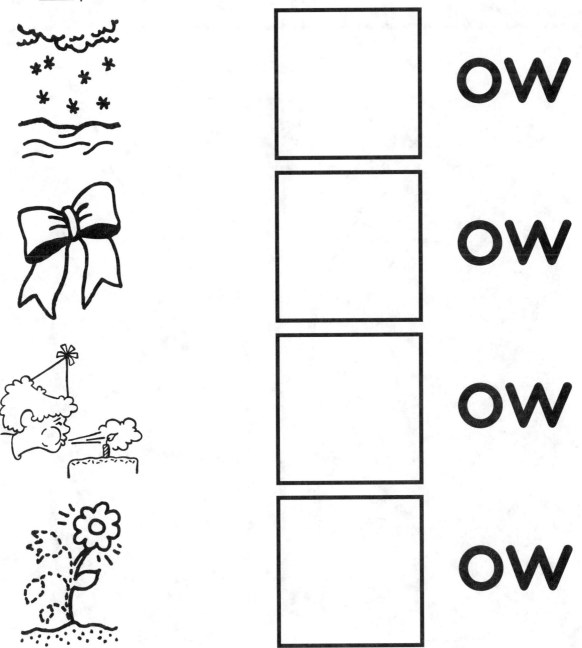

Mystery Picture

Color the spaces with **–oat** purple to discover the mystery picture. Color the other spaces blue.

Where's my purple _____?

Mystery Picture

Color the spaces with **–oke** gray to discover the mystery picture. Color the other spaces green.

I dislike _____ !

Mystery Picture

Color the spaces with **–ow** brown to discover the mystery picture. Color the other spaces blue.

I have a huge _____ boat.

Word Search

Find and color the **–oat** words.

| boat | coat | goat | gloat | float | throat |

c	b	o	a	t	d	p	c
g	l	o	a	t	m	f	o
h	a	f	n	i	t	e	a
t	r	e	a	c	i	n	t
i	g	o	a	t	u	b	i
n	e	t	h	r	o	a	t
f	l	o	a	t	e	a	e

Write the **–oat** words that you have found above.

_____   _____   _____

_____   _____   _____

Word Search

Find and color the **–oke** words.

poke	woke	yoke	broke	smoke	spoke

p	o	k	e	g	h	t	s
r	b	r	o	k	e	t	m
i	m	s	p	o	k	e	o
g	e	q	a	k	g	e	k
h	y	o	k	e	h	e	e
t	n	i	g	h	t	z	k
f	l	i	w	o	k	e	e

Write the **–oke** words that you have found above.

_____   _____   _____

_____   _____   _____

Word Search

Find and color the **–ow** words.

bow	row	tow	blow	grow	snow

l	s	p	g	n	e	e	t
i	m	c	r	n	e	t	o
n	b	l	o	w	p	s	w
e	e	r	w	r	t	l	h
n	i	o	e	a	u	e	i
b	o	w	s	n	o	w	n
h	f	s	v	i	n	e	e

Write the **–ow** words that you have found above.

_____   _____   _____

_____   _____   _____

_____   _____   _____

_____   _____   _____

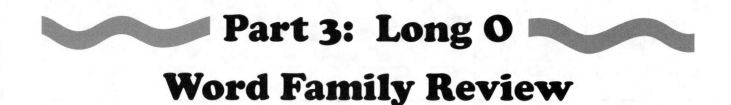

Part 3: Long O
Word Family Review

Activity Directions

Word Sort (pages 177 and 178)

Students will sort words in the correct columns.

(*Extension:* Have students read the words to classmates.)

Make, Read, and Write Long Vowel Word (page 179)

Students cut out the letter and picture cards on the dashed lines. Students manipulate letter cards to form words. Students then read the words and find the matching pictures. Lastly, students may use blank paper to write the words they have formed. Use plastic baggies or envelopes to store letters and pictures.

Long Vowel Fluency Practice (page 180)

Students read the randomly placed "long o" words from left to right. Sand timers may be given to students to time how many words they can read in the given time.

My Own Long Vowel Words (page 181)

Students will write their own "long o" words on the solid lines provided. They can read and share their words with classmates.

(*Note:* Students can also cut on the lines to make flashcards.)

Making Sentences with Long O Words (page 182, 183, or 184)

Students will cut out the "long o" words and glue them in the boxes to make sentences. They can use the picture clues. Students should be encouraged to read their sentences aloud.

 # Word Sort

1. Cut out the **long o** words.

2. Glue each word in the correct column on the following page.

3. Be careful! There are some words that do not belong to the word families.
   Can you find them?

bow	poke	woke	top	snow
dog	row	mop	boat	yoke
spoke	fog	tow	broke	chop
stop	coat	smoke	blow	shop
goat	gloat	float	throat	grow

-ow	-oat	-oke

Make, Read, and Write
Long Vowel Words

Cut out the dashed lines. Make, read and write **long o** words.

o	t	s	c	e
w	t	n	f	y
b	l	a	p	m
r	g	h	k	

Long Vowel Fluency Practice

← Read ← Read ← Read

bow	tow	blow	grow	snow
				boat
coat	goat	gloat	float	throat
				poke
woke	yoke	broke	smoke	spoke
				bow
poke	row	coat	woke	tow
				goat
boat	blow	gloat	broke	grow
				float
yoke				bow

My Own Long Vowel Words (long o)

181

Making Sentences with Long O Words

Cut out the **–oat** words below. Glue them in the correct boxes to create sentences. Read the sentences aloud.

1. The big ____ is at sea.

2. I can ____ on the water.

3. The doctor looked at my ____.

4. I hope he does not ____

- -

gloat	throat	boat	float

Making Sentences with Long O Words

Cut out the **–oke** words below. Glue them in the correct boxes to create sentences. Read the sentences aloud.

1. The rooster  me up.

2. Do you smell ?

3. The fancy shell  .

4. Please do not me.

poke   woke   smoke   broke

Making Sentences with Long O Words

Cut out the **-ow** words below. Glue them in the correct boxes to create sentences. Read the sentences aloud.

1. We need to ⬚ the car.

2. When will it ⬚ ?

3. The ⬚ is pretty.

4. ⬚ out the candles.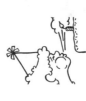

snow   bow   tow

Blow

Long U*

-ue

-ure

-ute

* The "long u" vowel has several phonetic sounds. The /ü/ as in *flute* and the /yü/ as in *cute* are included in this book.

Part 1: Long U
Teacher Support/Home Support

Activity Directions

Flashcards (pages 187 and 188, pages 189 and 190, or 191 and 192)

Copy the set of flashcards that you want the students to learn back to back (pages 187 and 188, pages 189 and 190, or pages 191 and 192). Make sure the cards align properly when copying.

Have students trace and rewrite "long u" words on side A along with reading the words aloud. Side B will allow students to draw their own interpretations of the words. Students will then cut out the cards and place them on a ring for review or use them as a reference.

Letter Slide (page 193, 194, or 195)

Teacher precuts dashed lines inside pictures. Students will cut the strips of letters. Students insert the letter strips to create and manipulate "long u" words.

(*Note:* Students can independently ask other classmates to read the words created with the letter slide.)

Blending Boxes (page 196, 197, or 198)

First, inform students that they will be building words by listening for beginning, middle, and ending sounds. Next, the teacher stretches out the word. Both student and teacher repeat the word slowly. Then, the teacher will ask questions to help guide students to develop the sounds to write in the proper boxes. Lastly, students blend the sounds while connecting the dots to show directionality. Students read the words and practice writing them on the line.

Beginning Sound Substitution (page 199, 200, or 201)

Students cross out the beginning sound to create a new "long u" word. Use the pictures on the left as a guide. Have students read the words as they create them. Teacher must inform students that they are only substituting the beginning sound to create a new word.

*The "long u" vowel has several phonetic sounds. The /ü/ as in *flute* and the /yü/ as in *cute* are included in this book.

clue

due

flue

Sue

glue

blue

due

clue

Sue

flue

blue

glue

cure

sure

I have no doubts.

lure

pure

100% NATURAL PEARS

cure

sure

lure

pure

cute

mute

jute

chute

lute

flute

cute

mute

jute

chute

lute

flute

Letter Slide

Cut the strip of letters. Cut the slits on the glue. Insert the strip of letters to create and manipulate the **–ue** words.

_____ue

gl
d
S
bl
cl
fl

Letter Slide

Cut the strip of letters. Cut the slits on the medicine bottle. Insert the strip of letters to create and manipulate the **–ure** words.

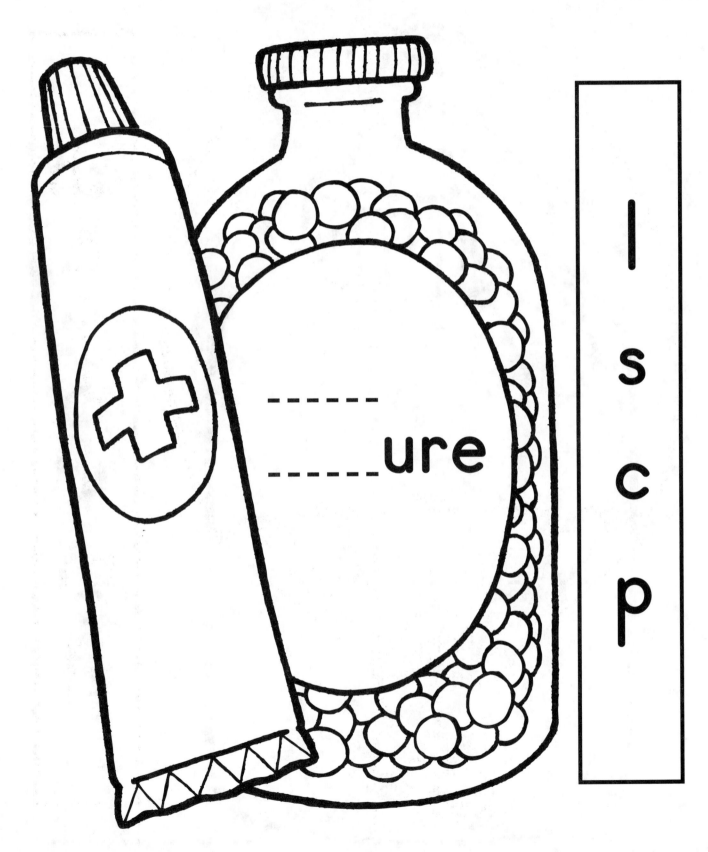

```
------
------ure
```

l
s
c
p

Letter Slide

Cut the strip of letters. Cut the slits on the parachute. Insert the strip of letters to create and manipulate the **–ute** words.

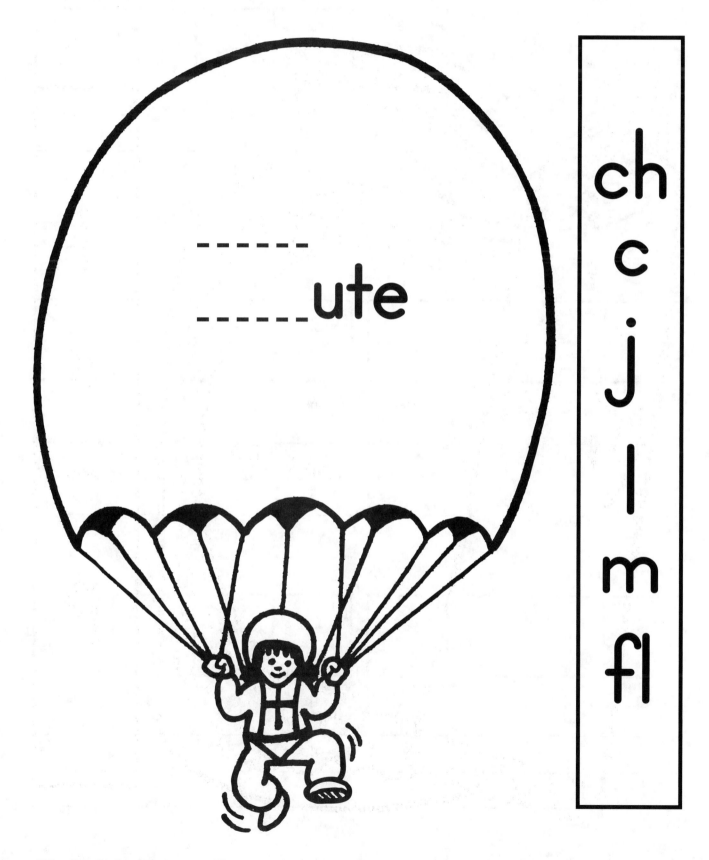

_____ute

ch
c
j
l
m
fl

Blending Boxes

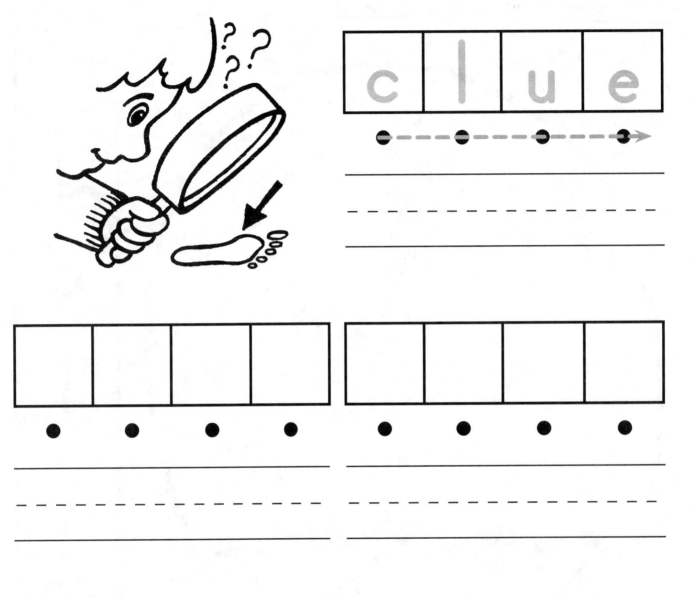

c	l	u	e

Blending Boxes

c	u	t	e

Blending Boxes

c	u	r	e

Beginning Sound Substitution

Cross out the beginning sound to create a new **–ue** word. Use the pictures on the left as a guide.

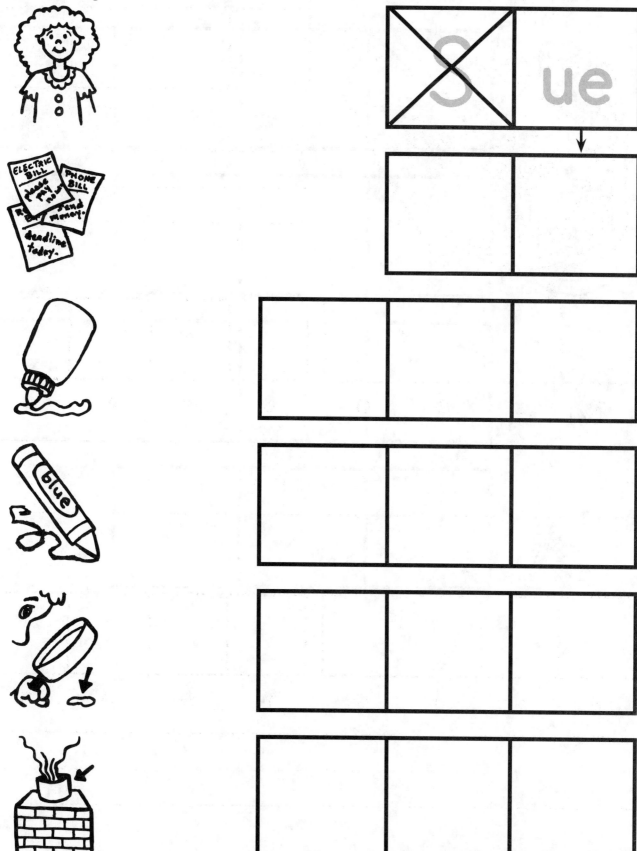

Beginning Sound Substitution

Cross out the beginning sound to create a new **–ure** word. Use the pictures on the left as a guide.

Beginning Sound Substitution

Cross out the beginning sound to create a new **–ute** word. Use the pictures on the left as a guide.

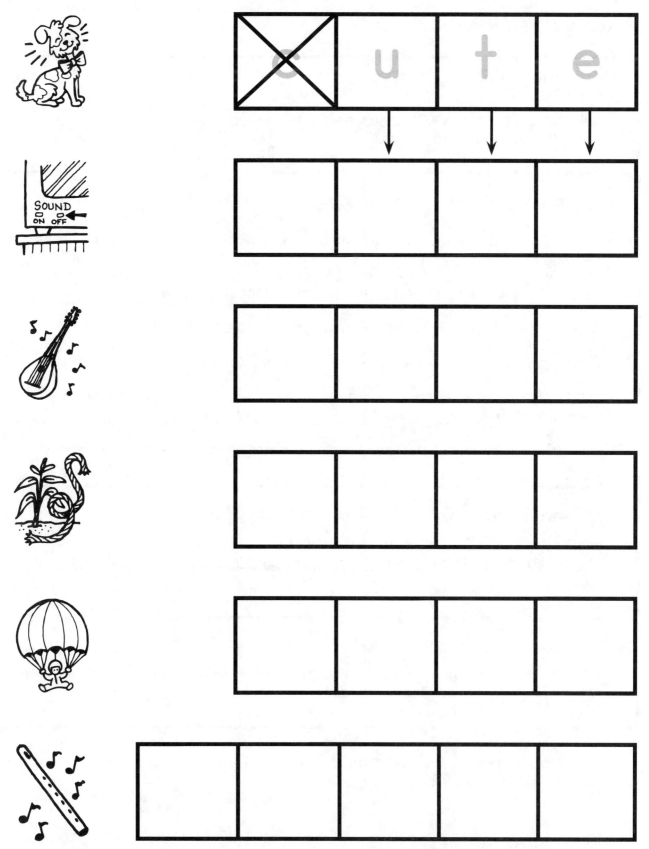

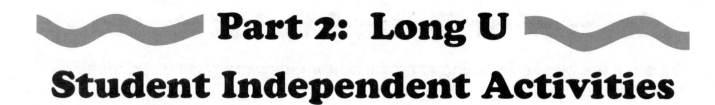

Part 2: Long U
Student Independent Activities

Activity Directions

Building Words (page 203, 204, or 205)

Cut out the letter boxes. Glue the letters in the correct boxes to create words that match the corresponding pictures.

Flip Book (pages 206–208 for *–ue*, pages 209–211 for *–ure*, pages 212–214 for *–ute*)

Copy page 2 and the "My Picture" page back to back. Make sure the dashed lines are aligned. Then copy page 1.

First, fold page 2 along the solid line and only cut the dashed lines.

Second, cut and glue the pictures from page 1 onto the flip book (page 2).

Third, have students draw their own pictures where it says "My Picture" in the inside.

Fourth, cut out the letter boxes from page 1. Glue letters to the corresponding pictures to make the correct words.

Fifth, have students write the words two more times.

Mystery Picture (page 215, 216, or 217)

Find and color the "long u" words to discover the mystery picture. Once the mystery picture is discovered, students will then write the "long u" mystery word in the sentence below.

Word Search (page 218, 219, or 220)

Find and color the "long u" words. Have students write the "long u" words that are found in the word search in the empty spaces below.

*The "long u" vowel has several phonetic sounds. The /ü/ as in *flute* and the /yü/ as in *cute* are included in this book.

Building Words

Cut out the letters below. Glue them in the correct boxes to create words that match the **–ue** pictures.

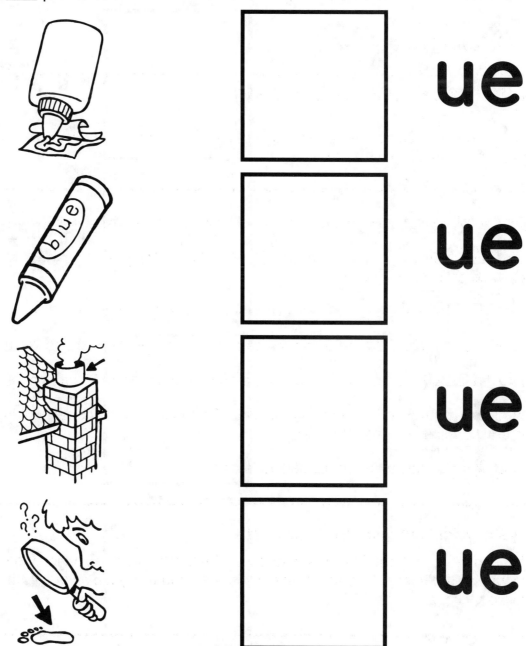

Building Words

Cut out the letters below. Glue them in the correct boxes to create words that match the **–ute** pictures.

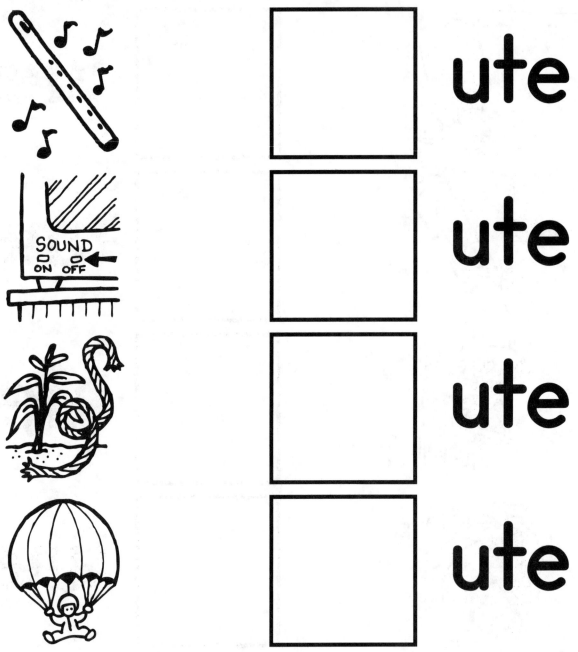

ute

ute

ute

ute

ch   fl   m   j

Building Words

Cut out the letters below. Glue them in the correct boxes to create words that match the **–ure** pictures.

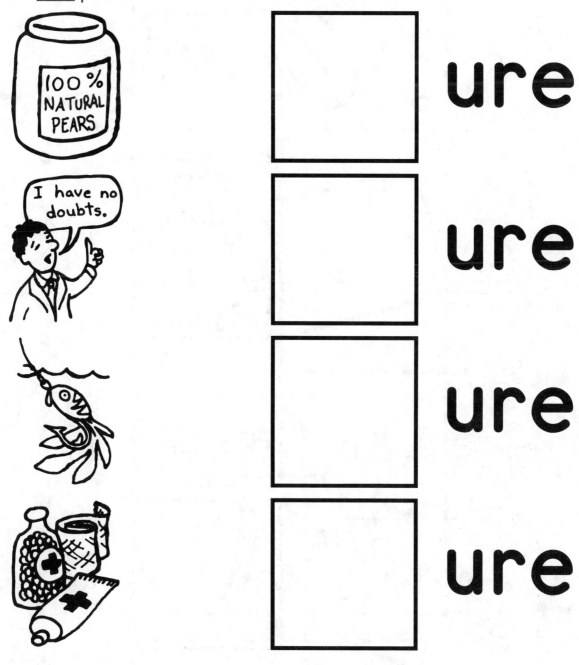

ure

ure

ure

ure

c   p   s   l

Flip Book (-ue)

Cut out the pictures and letters below.

Glue them on the flip book.

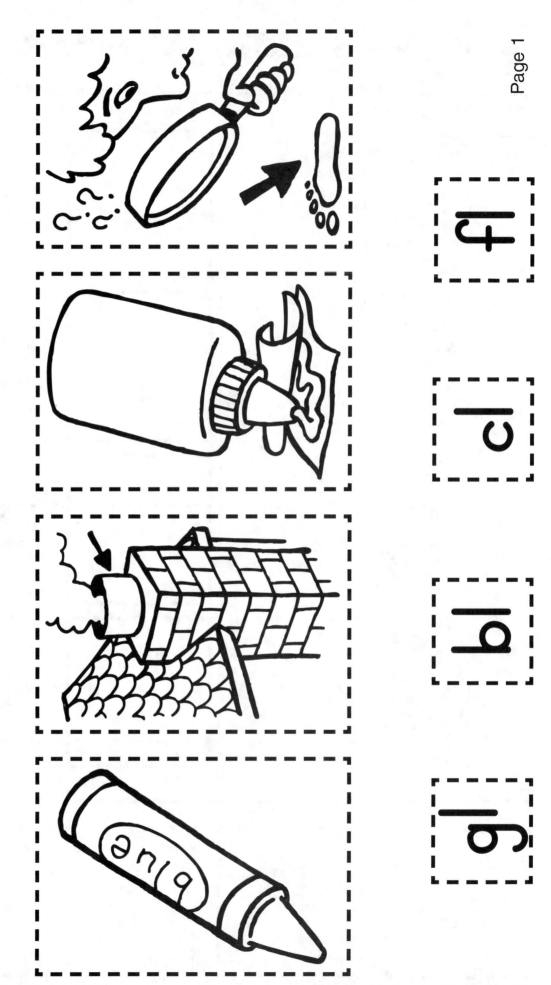

206

Page 2

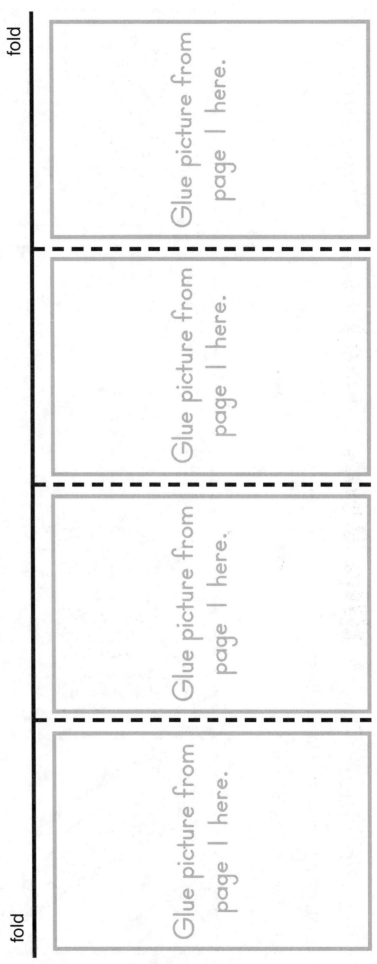

fold

Glue picture from page 1 here.

Glue picture from page 1 here.

Glue picture from page 1 here.

Glue picture from page 1 here.

fold

My Picture

My Picture

My Picture

My Picture

ue

ue

ue

ue

fold

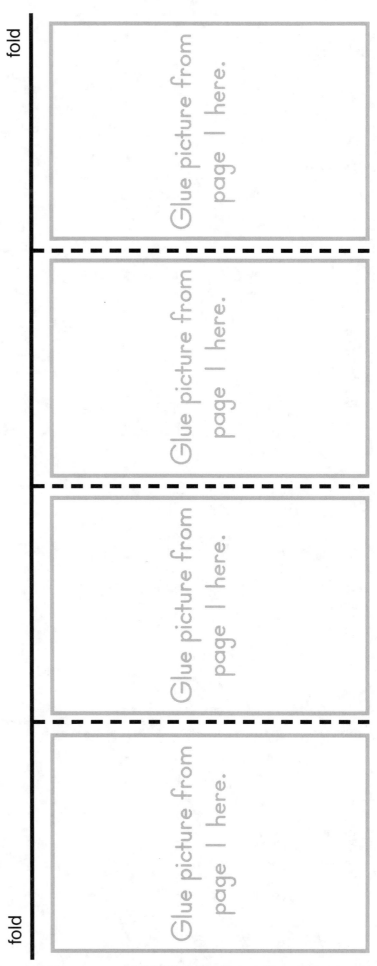

Glue picture from page 1 here.

Glue picture from page 1 here.

Glue picture from page 1 here.

Glue picture from page 1 here.

fold

My Picture

My Picture

My Picture

My Picture

ure

ure

ure

ure

Flip Book (–ure)

Cut out the pictures and letters below.

Glue them on the flip book.

Flip Book (–ute)

Cut out the pictures and letters below.

Glue them on the flip book.

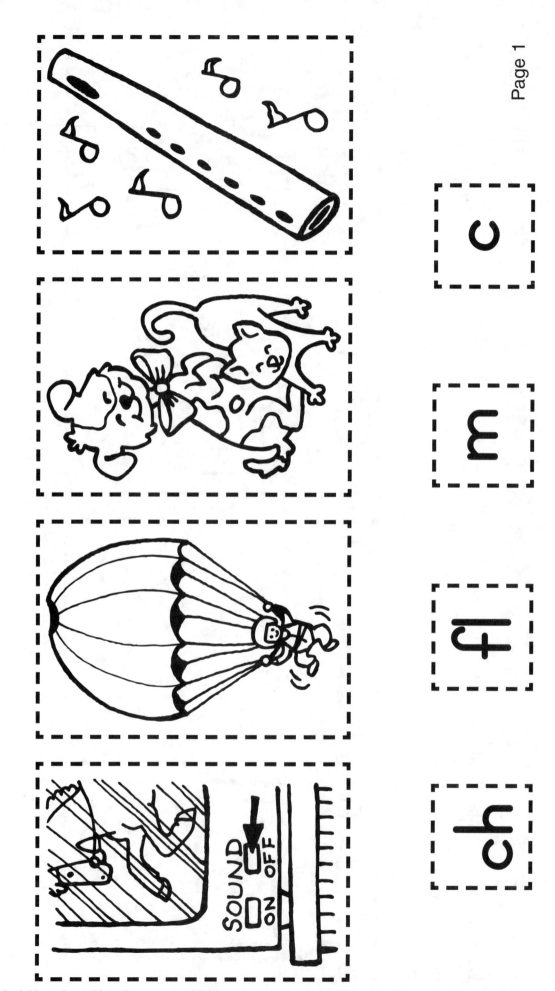

212

fold

Glue picture from page 1 here.

Glue picture from page 1 here.

Glue picture from page 1 here.

Glue picture from page 1 here.

fold

My Picture

My Picture

My Picture

My Picture

ute

ute

ute

ute

Mystery Picture

Color the spaces with **–ue** yellow to discover the mystery picture. Color the other spaces blue.

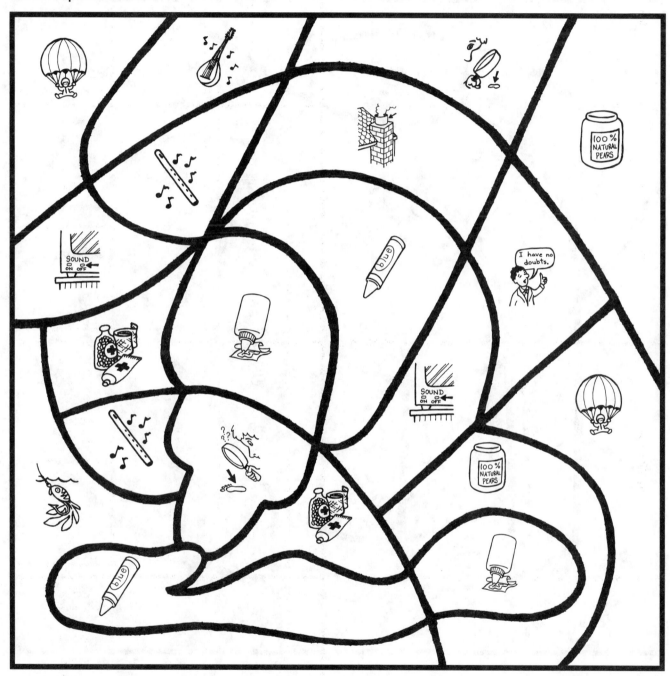

They lost their sticky _____.

Mystery Picture

Color the spaces with **–ure** orange to discover the mystery picture. Color the other spaces blue.

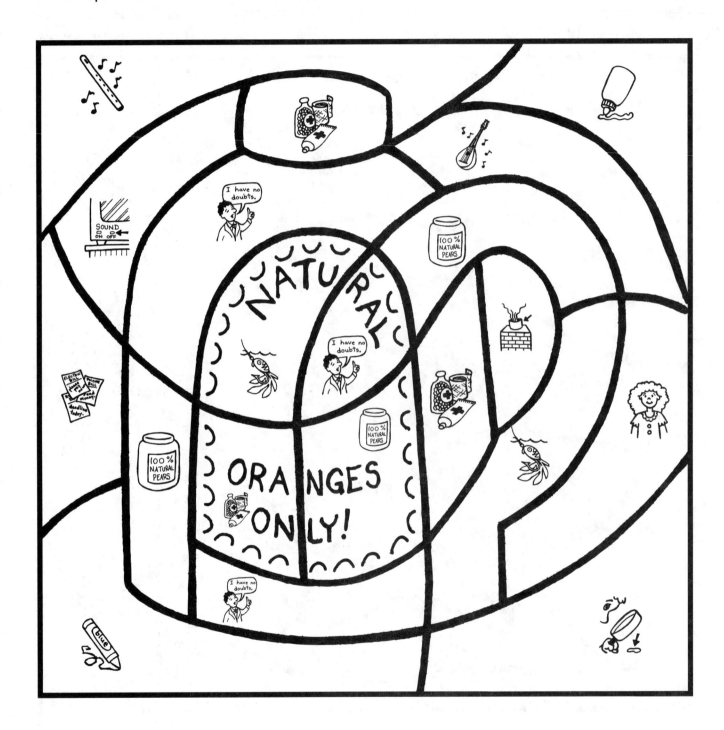

I drink 100%_____ juice.

Mystery Picture

Color the spaces with **–ute** red to discover the mystery picture. Color the other spaces blue.

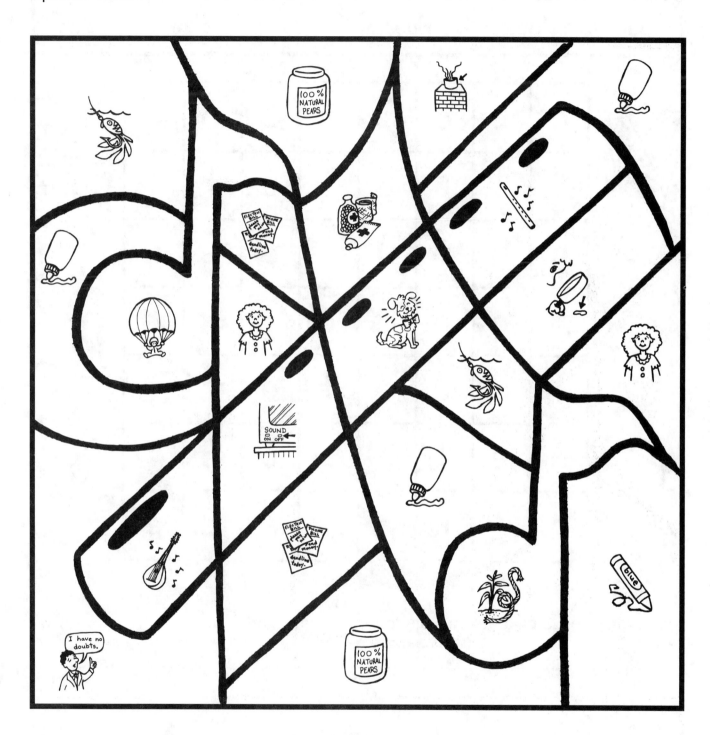

Hear me play the_____.

Word Search

Find and color the **–ue** words.

due	Sue	flue	clue	glue	blue

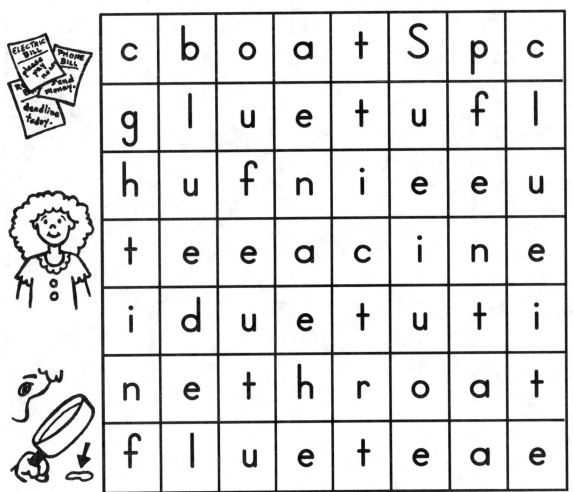

c	b	o	a	t	S	p	c
g	l	u	e	t	u	f	l
h	u	f	n	i	e	e	u
t	e	e	a	c	i	n	e
i	d	u	e	t	u	t	i
n	e	t	h	r	o	a	t
f	l	u	e	t	e	a	e

Write the **–ue** words that you have found above.

_____   _____   _____

_____   _____   _____

Word Search

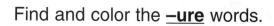

Find and color the **–ure** words.

cure	lure	pure	sure

l	s	u	r	e	t	e	p
i	m	c	r	n	e	t	u
n	b	l	u	r	e	s	r
e	e	u	w	r	t	l	e
n	i	n	e	a	u	e	i
c	u	r	e	n	o	w	n
h	f	s	v	i	n	e	e

Write the **–ure** words that you have found above.

_____   _____

_____   _____

_____   _____

_____   _____

Word Search

Find and color the **–ute** words.

cute	jute	lute	mute	chute	flute

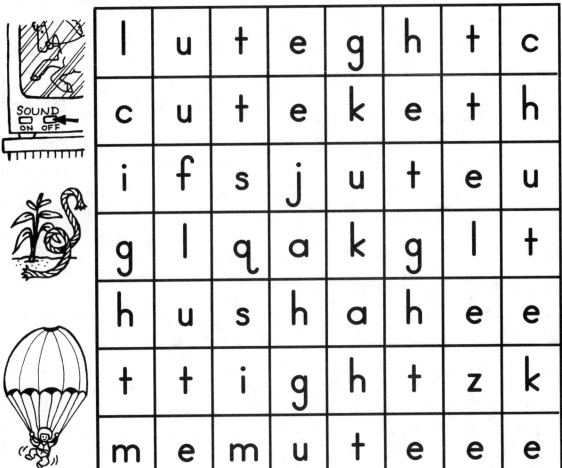

l	u	t	e	g	h	t	c
c	u	t	e	k	e	t	h
i	f	s	j	u	t	e	u
g	l	q	a	k	g	l	t
h	u	s	h	a	h	e	e
t	t	i	g	h	t	z	k
m	e	m	u	t	e	e	e

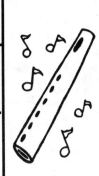

Write the **–ute** words that you have found above.

_____   _____   _____

- - - - - - - - -   - - - - - - - - -   - - - - - - - - -

_____   _____   _____

- - - - - - - - -   - - - - - - - - -   - - - - - - - - -

_____   _____   _____

- - - - - - - - -   - - - - - - - - -   - - - - - - - - -

Part 3: Long U
Word Family Review

Activity Directions

Word Sort (pages 222 and 223)

Students will sort words in the correct columns.

(*Extension:* Have students read the words to classmates.)

Make, Read, and Write Long Vowel Words (page 224)

Students cut out the letter and picture cards on the dashed lines. Students manipulate letter cards to form words. Students then read the words and find the matching pictures. Lastly, students may use blank paper to write the words they have formed. Use plastic baggies or envelopes to store letters and pictures.

Long Vowel Fluency Practice (page 225)

Students read the randomly placed "long u" words from left to right. Sand timers may be given to students to time how many words they can read in the given time.

My Own Long Vowel Words (page 226)

Students will write their own "long u" words on the lines provided. They can read and share their words with classmates.

(*Note:* Students can also cut on the solid lines to make flashcards.)

Making Sentences with Long U Words (page 227, 228, or 229)

Students will cut out the "long u" words and glue them in the boxes to make sentences. They can use the picture clues. Students should be encouraged to read their sentences aloud.

*The "long u" vowel has several phonetic sounds. The /ü/ as in *flute* and the /yü/ as in *cute* are included in this book.

Word Sort

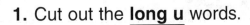

1. Cut out the <u>**long u**</u> words.

2. Glue each word in the correct column on the following page.

3. Be careful! There are some words that do not belong to the word families. Can you find them?

cure	flute	Sue	shut	cute
mute	lure	run	flue	bus
pure	rut	blue	cup	jute
chute	due	nut	glue	gum
sure	mug	clue	bug	lute

-ue	-ute	-ure

Make, Read, and Write
Long Vowel Words

Cut on the dashed lines. Make, read, and write **long u** words.

d	u	e	s	b
l	c	f	g	r
p	t	j	m	c
h	ch	S		

Long Vowel Fluency Practice

Read →   Read →   Read →   Read →

due	Sue	blue	clue	flue	glue	cute
jute	mute	lute	chute	flute	cure	pure
sure	lure	due	cute	cure	Sue	jute
pure	blue	lute	sure	clue	mute	lure
flue	chute	glue	flute	due	sure	blue

My Own Long Vowel Words (long u)

226

Making Sentences with Long U Words

Cut out the **-ue** words below. Glue them in the correct boxes to create sentences. Read the sentences aloud.

1. My project is [   ] today.

2. We found [   ] number two.

3. The truck is dark [   ].

4. I ran out of [   ].

Making Sentences with Long U Words

Cut out the –ute words below. Glue them in the correct boxes to create sentences. Read the sentences aloud.

1. The [ ] will open.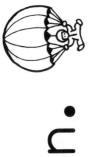

2. I enjoy playing the [ ].

3. My puppy is very [ ].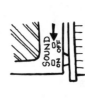

4. Where is the [ ] button?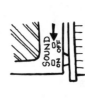

cute | chute | mute | flute

Making Sentences with Long U Words

Cut out the **–ure** words below. Glue them in the correct boxes to create sentences. Read the sentences aloud.

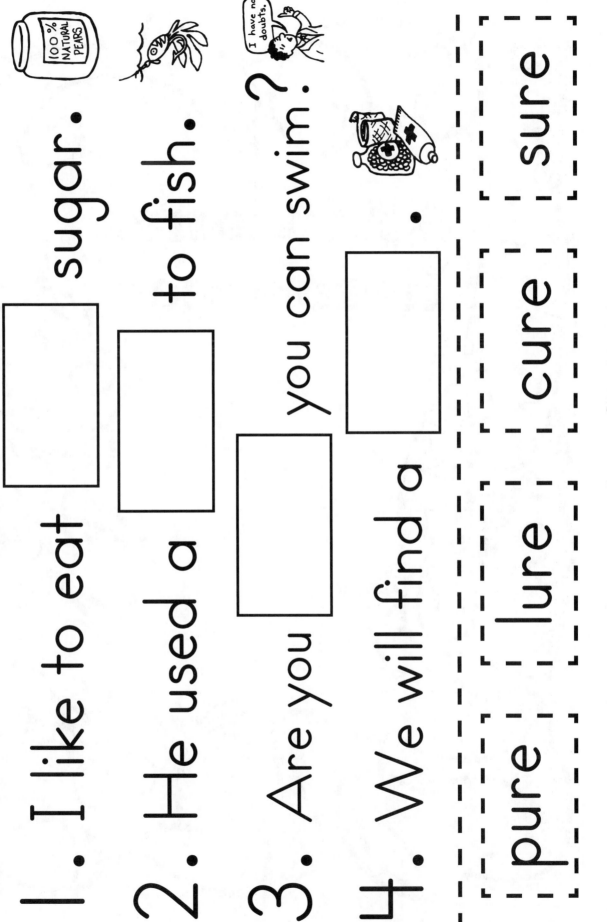

1. I like to eat ⬚ sugar.

2. He used a ⬚ to fish.

3. Are you ⬚ you can swim?

4. We will find a ⬚ .

pure | lure | cure | sure

Additional Resources

Blending Boxes

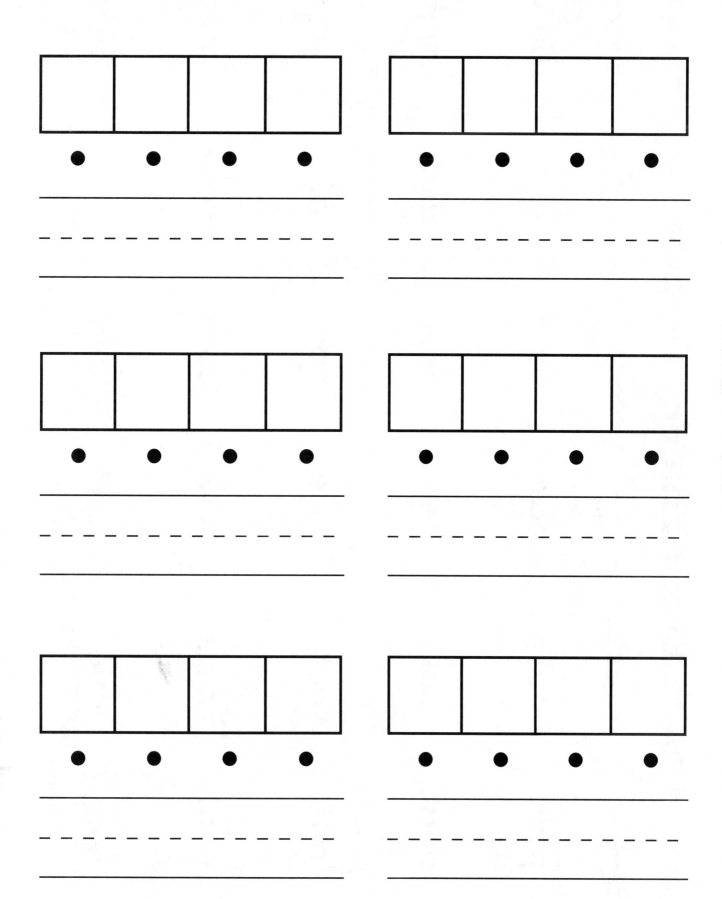

Mixed Fluency Practice

Read → Read → Read →

pain	cake	day	beat	line	bow
boat	poke	bee	deep	dice	knight
due	cute	cure	rain	lake	ray
heat	nine	row	coat	woke	knee
jeep	mice	light	Sue	jute	pure

Mixed Fluency Practice

Read →   Read →   Read →

brain	rake	say	meat	pine	tow
goat	yoke	see	weep	rice	night
blue	lute	sure	chain	flake	gray
seat	vine	blow	gloat	broke	tee
sleep	price	right	clue	mute	lure

Mixed Fluency Practice

→ Read → Read → Read

Spain	shake	play	treat	shine	grow
float	smoke	tree	steep	slice
bright	flew	chute	train	snake
spray	wheat	spine	snow	throat
spoke	three	sweep	ice	flight	glue

234

Mixed Fluency Practice

→ Read   → Read   → Read   → Read

flute	pain	bee	cake	deep	day
dice	beat	knight	line	due	bow
cute	boat	cure	poke	rain	knee
lake	jeep	ray	mice	heat	light
nine	Sue	row	jute	coat	pure

Mixed Fluency Practice

Read → Read → Read → Read

woke	brain	see	rake	weep	say
rice	meat	night	pine	blue	tow
lute	goat	sure	yoke	chain	tee
lake	sleep	gray	price	seat	right
vine	clue	blow	mute	gloat	lure

Mixed Fluency Practice

← Read → Read → Read

broke	Spain	tree	shake	steep
play	slice	treat	bright	shine	flew
grow	chute	float	smoke	train
three	snake	sweep	spray	ice	wheat
flight	spine	glue	snow	flute	throat

Mixed Fluency Practice

Read → Read → Read →

spoke	pain	day	tow	goat	broke
vine	blue	mute	cure	boat	bow
line	woke	pure	lute	yoke	grow
spine	snow	nine	clue	cute	sure
poke	float	row	lure	Sue	gloat

Word Family Bingo

	FREE	

My Own Long Vowel Words